The Colours of Me

Compiled by
Kez Wickham St George & Michelle Weitering

AN MMH PRESS ANTHOLOGY

Published by MMH Press 2021
Copyright © 2021 Kez Wickham St George & Michelle Weitering

All Rights Reserved. No part of this book may be used or reproduced by any means, graphic, electronic, or mechanical, including photocopying, recording, taping or by any information storage retrieval system without the written permission of the copyright owner except in the case of brief quotations embodied in critical articles and reviews.

Because of the dynamic nature of the Internet, any web addresses or links contained in this book may have changed since publication and may no longer be vaild. The views expressed in this work are solely those of the author and do not necessarily reflect the views of the publisher and the publisher hereby disclaims any responsibility for them.

 A catalogue record for this work is available from the National Library of Australia

National Library of Australia
Cataloguing-in-Publication data:

The Colours of Me/MMH Press

ISBN: 978-0-6451483-8-1
(paperback)

ISBN: 978-0-6451483-9-8
(ebook)

Foreword
by Karen Mc Dermott

The Colours of Me anthology, compiled by MMH Press' author duo Michelle Weitering and Kez Wickham St George, is a collective vision of genius that attracted the perfect authors into this book.

Readers will have so many beautiful takeaways this book that doesn't hold back on the 'feels'.

Not only does my own sister show up as a guest contributor sharing her IVF story, but there are also many other amazing women, some of who I know and some who I have yet to meet.

Each story will bring the reader on a soul-fuelled journey that will leave a mark on their heart. For many of us, we will feel not alone, for others we will feel blessed that we have not had to endure that shade of colour in our lifetime, but collectively this book has the power to bring understanding and insights to the hearts and minds of others and create deeper empathy and understanding that we truly don't know what is going on behind the scenes for others so be kind when you can, it makes a real difference.

The Colours of Me anthology is an absolute must-read for everyone who wants to know more.

Colours of Me

My heart was heavy its strings sang with grief
family and friends now parted
my questions or how and why not so brief
New friends dried my tears words of wisdom uttered
Relax and look inside of you, the answer is there to see

I saw my spirit dance with joy one of love and grace
I watched amazed at its flight and pace
My true colours I now know this is not denied
Oceans of indigo with forests of green
Blue skies that fill the eye
A deep understanding flows in my blood not the questions of where or why
I emerged from a woman who lay cocoon curled
Awakening to my life of beauty life is what I make of it
not of others emotional surging
For I am a woman of many strong passions now not caring if others don't see
For it's my spirit that now knows the difference
To by true to The Colours of Me

- Kez Wickham St George

Contents

The Roll of a Dice
by Emma Weaver 1

This is Me
by Kez Wickham St George 11

From My Heart to Your Heart
by Di Riddell 23

How I Learned to Love My Shadow
by Amanda Schubert 36

Are You Listening Now?
by Danielle Aitken 48

Building Dreams, Finding Strength
by Sue Croft 61

Thriving – Moving Beyond Trauma
by Jacquie Walker 74

Tribute to an Angel
by Michelle Weitering 85

The Balance of Colour in Conscious & Subconscious
by Melissa Billman 99

Becoming Me
by Patricia Lovell 111

Imperfect
by Toni Lontis 125

A Pivot
by Sonee Singh 138

Letter from 'The Lucky One'
by Lindy Wyse 151

When Demons Breathe New Perspective
by Rachel Francis 163

Love & Loss on the Way to Mammyville
by Joanne Henry 175

Colour Matching
by Julia Kaylock 186

Peeling Back the Layers
by Holly Rose Holland 198

This Crazy Journey Called 'Life'
by Jodie Satie 209

The Roll of a Dice

by Emma Weaver

Life can take you on many journeys, and one thing is for sure, it happens to us all and can come so unexpectedly. How you deal with change and new situations is what builds your resilience and becomes part of you. I have been faced with many challenges in my life. After many twists and turns along the way, each experience has changed me, making me stronger and raising my vibration in the world and showing me a higher purpose.

Becoming a young mum, I was grief-stricken when my daughter's dad was killed in a traffic accident. As a mum already to two beautiful children when I met and fell in love again, I was living the dream. Everything was going so well. We decided to add to our family to bind it together.

We decided early on that we wanted to have a child. The yearning was there, the excitement was real and the hope filled our lives. With enthusiasm, passion, and love we set about making magic happen. After one month went by, I laughed that we thought it would happen straight away. We were both healthy people, my cycle was regular, and we could see no obstacles. Six months later and still we had no success, so conversations started. Perhaps we need to time this better, be more aware of fertile days. We purchased an ovulation kit, the first step on the road of the whole thing becoming less romantic and very clinical.

Every month I could feel the disappointment, the pain and the grief of not being successful. As the months added up and became a year, more action had to be taken. Two family members were now pregnant, and excitement had begun for their journeys, so we kept quiet about ours. It can be such a private matter and an internal battle of feelings. I wondered, what is wrong with me that this is not happening for us?

The realisation was now starting to set in that this was not happening. My internal voice shook with panic, and I started to question everything. We decided to do some research and take things a little further and try something different. We read books, watched podcasts, and listened to ever-changing opinions on what was best to do and not do. Loose male underwear, herbal remedies, reflexology acupuncture, legs in the air, positioning, waiting until the time of the month was just right, and lots more; we tried everything. The romance was taken out of the equation and it became a numbers game.

Days of ovulation, days of sperm, favourable days to conceive; all of this became part of our daily life.

We reached the twenty-month mark feeling vulnerable and at a complete loss. I contacted our GP, who referred us to a consultant. This was not an easy appointment, we had to discuss everything about ourselves, my cycles, how long we had been trying, our medical histories. We then had to go for every test imaginable, both internally and externally.

Another appointment to the fertility clinic revealed that this was just not going to happen naturally for us. We found this particularly hard to let sink in, even though we knew by now that we were unable to conceive on our own, that we would need assistance. Every emotion comes to the fore: shock, disappointment, disbelief, sadness, grief, anger – our heads were spinning.

I decided to do some research and developed a sense of the enormity of fertility issues and how it can impact couples and individuals.

On 25 July 1978 history was made, bringing hope and options for those who previously thought it was impossible. This was the day the first IVF baby was born – a healthy baby girl, Louise Brown.

Since then, over five million babies have been born through IVF. Millions of people wanting to become parents but were unable to do so, whether it was due to male or female infertility, couples in same-sex relationships, or being a single person; many have gone through this process to achieve their dream of having a baby, becoming a parent, and feeling complete.

The dictionary describes the cycle of life as a series of changes in the life of an organism, including reproduction. One of the assumptions that people make about life is that we will reproduce, and if not all, at least most of us. People assume that they will become a parent, that the ability to reproduce defines us.

One-sixth of the human population – just under 15% – is faced with fertility challenges. The emotional and mental impact of this is profound. We had options, although we felt robbed of the chance to conceive on our own and had to mourn the choices that had been taken away. But it was out of our hands. Our dreams were now in the hands of another.

There was a two-year wait for fertility treatment – imagine, this issue is so prevalent that there is a waiting list of two years! So many people are impacted and yet I had never heard anyone talk about it. This was all new to me. A two-year waiting list and only one health service available.

We decided this was our journey and we would not tell anyone what we were going through. We decided to go private and hopefully be successful within the two years, while waiting for our turn in the health care system. No one knew we were trying for a baby, and when anyone was insensitive enough to ask when we would be adding to our family, we brushed it off, saying work was too busy. Little did anyone know what we were going through, these comments were so unhelpful.

The two-hour journey to the closest clinic was a strange one, we were nervous and excited as we spoke about what we thought was going to happen and ran away with ourselves thinking of outcomes and time scales. The feelings are real, and hope is what keeps you going.

More tests, bloods, examinations, and deep conversations about my body. Conversations I have never had with myself, never mind others. I was now starting to feel like a vessel, not a human. It was very clinical and all about body parts.

After a while it was determined that we would have a procedure called ICSI. This is where they put the sperm directly into the retrieved egg to ensure contact, leaving nothing to chance.

A schedule was drafted, and we had to then pay in advance for all the injections and suppositories. Then we waited for my menstrual cycle that month, everything was meticulously planned around that. It's a numbers game after all.

Along came my period, it is strange this roller-coaster. Before this, I would pray every month for my period not to come. Now, I was praying that it would hurry up and come so that we could start our ICSI cycle.

This journey is full of paradoxes. What you think should happen is the one thing you do not want to happen, it's all about assisting nature to take its course. It can be hard to get your head around the process. A lot of people have an opinion on this process, however it is so personal that each person or couple should be allowed to make their own informed choice.

I embarked on the cycle of injections, finding them particularly hard, they stung and I had to dig very deep, once in the morning and once in the afternoon. My day revolved around these injections; they were constantly on my mind. I tried everything to make them sting less: ice cubes, pulling an elastic band to distract me, and many other tactics before finding that chewing gum helped. Hey, whatever works!

I was now feeling more isolated, still deciding not to tell anyone, we decided to keep going it alone. I made several journeys up and down to the clinic – it was a four-hour round trip – to see if my ovaries have been stimulated by the injections to create follicles. The key is to create as many favourable ones as possible without overstimulating, then waiting for them to trigger, which is, yes of course, another injection. All this was happening while I was working and attending family events, trying to suppress my emotions and feeling very vulnerable – which was a new feeling for me. You really must look after your wellbeing throughout this journey and that is not something that is spoken about; perhaps you might read it in a leaflet.

The weight of all of this started to show within our relationship and tension was rising. Talking about it was painful; not talking about it was painful too. My tummy now felt like a pin cushion, skinny jeans were too uncomfortable to wear; dresses and skirts were my only option. Whilst this may seem trivial, in the grand scheme of things it was yet another option taken away from me.

Egg retrieval day came, and I was now overstimulated. We retrieved lots of eggs which was a good thing, and my partner dispensed his offering so that ICSI could take place. All was well at that end. It's not all about the woman; men go through this too.

We had eighteen beautiful A-grade embryos. The aim was to grow them to blastocyst (day five). Each day we received a phone call to say how they were doing, and we really felt that our babies were alive. You become attached and get upset when the numbers go down a little.

Due to my overstimulation they decided to freeze our blastocyst embryos. We were devastated as we had thought we were good to go. This is the roller-coaster of IVF; nothing is predictable, and you must let go of the controls as the decisions are ultimately out of your hands. The key is not to be so rigid about the process. I had it all worked out in my head, I even had the date of when the baby would possibly be due if all of this went to plan. This allowed me to hope and to dream of a positive outcome, which you need to keep going, however it is not helpful when things do not go exactly to plan – it can cause you more stress than you need. I learnt to let it go a bit, to trust the process and take it in stages.

Again, we waited for my menstrual cycle. When it arrived, we phoned in. The insemination procedure is strange, but you potentially get to see your baby conceived as they insert the embryo through a tube using an ultrasound as guidance. We watched the whole thing on a screen. Well, that was it, it was where it was meant to be. We must be pregnant!

The two-week wait is torture, you watch every part of your body, every twitch to see signs of pregnancy. I was going for walks and eating lots of pineapple because I read somewhere this helps the embryo to attach. I was determined to make sure I did everything right.

Two weeks later, the test was negative. We were absolutely devastated, and disbelieving, as we had seen the whole process. It is strange how we were so convinced, as after all, there is only a 20-35% chance of success after the first treatment. This increases with time until the chance of a successful pregnancy becomes 45-53% after three full cycles. Nonetheless, this news led to lots of disappointment and grief.

After a few months we decided to try again. I am not sure if it was better or worse knowing what lay ahead: injections, procedures and the two-week wait. We became more familiar with the nurses and the consultants and saw the familiar faces of other clients. I remember one day we were sitting in the waiting room and a couple came in with a toddler. We all just smiled at each other and watched in amusement as he entertained us with his playfulness. The mother of the young boy looked at us apologetically and said they often felt bad bringing him in as they know why people were there, and that they were going through the process again. Their little boy was an IVF baby, providing proof that it could work. This gave us more hope. I am not sure if we have ever knowingly met a child born through IVF – not that it matters, but we truly felt he was a miracle.

We went through the whole process again, with another negative result.

At this stage things were becoming strained. Two failed attempts and the accompanying heartache, we were tired of it all and decided to stop and take stock. People had already noticed that we were under strain, they could tell something was going on, and we wanted to keep our pain private.

A few weeks later when the NHS letter came to call us forward for free treatment, I actually could not believe it, it appeared in such a timely manner, yet we were still so raw. It was a little nudge saying, 'Go on, one more try, I know you can do this.'

After many lengthy discussions, we decided that this would be our last go. I think it is important to discuss how long you will try. We decided to do things a little differently. For a greater chance of success, we identified and eliminated all stressors from our lives: people, extra work, and situations that caused us unnecessary stress.

Down the same road we had to go, back to the start of the whole process. Even though we had embryos, we went through everything all over again.

I learnt to be kinder to myself, I rewarded myself every day for taking the injections. I would go to appointments on my own in the early hours of the morning and blast music for the whole four-hour journey, surrounding myself with good things. The waiting rooms were full, even at 7am, full of people on the same journey, with the same look on their faces; and still no-one talking.

Understanding how this all works, though, you do have to leave it to the professionals and hand over the power to them to get you pregnant. Faith, I think it is called. This helped me a lot as I was so methodical with the whole process and thinking things would go a certain way. I became very upset at times when they didn't. A life lesson learnt there, I feel.

On that day in August 2015, I was nervous. This was it for us, the strain was taking its toll and we were all-in. It was a lovely drive up to the city, no problem getting parked; we walked in to the all too familiar, packed waiting room, with new faces every time, we took our seat and waited to be called. I remember we took a picture of us sitting in the waiting room, not sure why, but we always wanted to keep memories of our journey regardless of the outcome.

When we were called, I was brought into a separate room to get gowned up in a not so flattering blue medical gown. Lying on the bed, legs high in the air, breathing in through my nose and out through my mouth, having general chitchat, the nurse confirmed my name and checked the catheter to ensure the proper embryos were waiting.

The doctor came in, didn't speak. We watched the screen as before and saw the line of the tube, and just like that, we saw a flash of white light. An unmistakable white flash. We looked at each other and smiled, acknowledging what we had just seen.

The doctor got up and said, 'Well that's that. Good luck.' Up I got and we headed home. The dreaded two-week wait was upon us …

I couldn't wait for the two weeks. After ten days I sneaked off to take a test. It was positive! I get goosebumps every time I say that. In 2016 our beautiful baby was born, all 9lb 6oz …

Looking back, I have learned so much. The experience has changed me as a person. How could it not? Be kind to everyone you meet as you truly do not know what people are going through.

I learned to show up for myself, not for others.

Sharing our stories and being true to who we are changes things. It allows us to connect with ourselves and with others going through similar situations. We all have many sides to us and different life experiences. We are evolving, changing, and learning all the time. It is our experiences that shape us and make us who we are. So, embrace it all, learn who you are, take time to know your values, your inner voice – and love all the colours of you.

Emma Weaver is the founder of Mental Wealth International, an organisation supporting businesses to achieve better mental health and wellbeing within the workplace. She is also an international bestselling author with her debut novel, *The Blue Line*.

As an international speaker, Emma uses her voice to champion causes close to her heart. Her purpose in life is to support people to have a voice and to create a safe platform where this can happen. Emma has over twenty-two years' experience working in the mental health and wellbeing sector. Motivated by her purpose, Emma provides hope and expertise to people through both her personal and professional skills and experiences. She has presented two TEDx talks, entitled 'Mental Wealth' and 'IVF - What's love got to do with it?' Emma has also won the 'Women to look up to 2021' award.

Emma currently resides in County Fermanagh, a beautiful rural county in Ireland. A native of Clones, Emma lives very close to her family homestead. She is a mother of three beautiful children, who are her world and her inspiration every day.

Emma is the ambassador for *The Colours of Me*.

This is Me
by Kez Wickham St George

The doctors and specialist told me that life would be fabulous after menopause; all the problems of the past, headaches, bloating, sleepless nights, and those awful hot flushes would be gone. I hung onto those words like they were the Holy Grail. I could not wait for it all to be over. There was no magical cure to what nature was allowing – it was a waiting game, and I was taken aback when I asked how long this was expected to go on. The answer: maybe five to ten years. Bloody hell! No one should have to go through this for ten years, this was awful.

Memories of my mother came flooding back as I walked home from the doctor's rooms that day. It was one of those days when silence was golden; usually I would take the busy footpath to go home as it was faster, but today I needed to breathe, to sort and to assemble my thoughts, so I chose the beach walk home which was longer and more picturesque.

The wind was so soft against my skin, the sun not yet hot enough to burn, the dark grey sand held onto my footprints as I wandered the shoreline. Finding a large rock to sit on, I watched the gentle waves wash in and out, they sounded like they were sighing, or as Mum would say, the calm before the storm. I smiled at that thought, how right she was, the calmness of my female body had begun to brew into a storm. Would I sink, or would I survive?

I remembered her struggle with menopause. I was a post-war child, with two older sisters in their teens by the time I was five years old. My father was my Superman, a jack of all trades and the man of the house in all ways. If Dad said jump, we would ask, 'How high?' When Mum began her journey into menopause, it was a not talked about, they just referred to it as *The Change*.

I was intrigued by it all, and when I asked, 'What was she going to change into?' I was smacked and told not to be so rude. Yes I know, smacking is not encouraged today, but in those days it was 'Duck, or you're gonna cop it'. This was New Zealand in the 1950s, and Mum was creative in all ways bar one: she was a shocking cook (sorry, Mum, but it's true – in saying that, your baking was to die for!). Mum was also a talented seamstress, poet, and songwriter. Come debutante or bridal season, she was a very popular lady and always booked out, her clients coming from all over the Wellington city district.

Both sides of my family married into different cultures. Friday night was the family night, many nations converged onto the Wickham household. Mum was always the bright sassy lady of the house, the entertainer, who would sing and dance with my aunties and cousins. Was it just me who noticed the black circles, the sudden bouts of tears, the lost look, the panic that I would see in her beautiful grey eyes? When the headaches became migraines, I was the one asked to brush her silvering hair with warm water and lavender oil, my small hands, clumsy and unsure, as she was in such pain, I did my best with as much love as I could muster in my little heart.

Dad did his best I guess; on her good days Mum shone, the house sparkled, she would laugh and sing, she would dance and skip with me, holding me close. The bad days were getting more common when she would lie in bed and cry, clutching her stomach, calling out for a hot water bottle and a cup of tea. Dad would say, 'Girls, help your Mum; I'm off to the pub.'

My two sisters would wait until he had gone, then kiss mum goodbye. 'Be well soon Mum,' they would say, and dash off. That left me, who at such a young age learnt very fast; if you were going to do something, do it properly. I learnt how to look after Mum. I learnt how to wash and dry dishes and clean up the toilet and bathroom after she had one of her vomiting sessions, often missing days of school to be her nurse. One day as I left for primary school, she was overly affectionate, holding onto me till it was uncomfortable – the look in her eyes made me uneasy. They found her comatose in Dad's workshop, kerosene had been ingested. An ambulance was called, and our local hospital alerted. Then, the long wait under the bright lights of the hospital corridors. The silent shoes of the nurses in their white uniforms were unsettling, doctors in white coats were quietly conferring with Dad; everyone was so serious and unhappy.

The silence that settled onto this once happy house was haunting.

I was marched into the lounge by my Dad, and the talking to he gave me made me scared that I had done something wrong. He knelt before me, placing his large work-worn hands on each of my arms. We were eye to eye, his blue eyes so stern as he said, 'It's not your fault, your Mum has a mental disorder, but you should have stayed with her.'

When I heard the word 'suicide', I asked Dad what that meant. He just stared at me. 'You're too young to understand.' I was ushered out of the room knowing, somehow, I was to blame. My two older sisters looked at me accusingly. One sister pinched me, 'I hate you.' The other one, hearing my sobs, cuddled me, 'You should have stayed with her.'

My dad, slumped in his chair, his hands covering his face, tears dripping between his fingers, was too sad to comfort me. That day would be etched on my mind forever. Yes, Mum survived, with many consequences; severe burning to her throat and intestines. Her menopause was forgotten for a while as she mended, Aspro and Valium the choice of medication. I was with Mum when the doctor suggested, 'Mrs Wickham, I would take up smoking, it will help calm your nerves, and maybe a sherry or two at night to help you sleep.' Mum puffed on her ciggies, had her sherry at night to help her sleep, and every morning her hands would tremble till the Aspro and Valium worked their magic.

Her dressmaking and song writing forgotten, Mum spent her days lying in haze of Valium and cigarettes. Dad worked all odd hours; he was the ink supervisor at a printing company, so he taught me how to cook simple dishes. If Mum was not capable, someone had to feed me. Porridge with condensed milk became my new best friend. When they took the medication away from her, bedlam became the norm in the house. Menopause returned, holding hands with jealousy. She accused Dad of having an affair with my aunty. My older sister was being ravaged by a man on the train. And I? Well, I was a much too inquisitive girl. 'Don't even think about kissing a boy till you're twenty-one or I will skin you alive.'

One by one, my sisters married and left home, each time there was a huge wedding and much drama. After they left, I was alone with Mum most days, treading on eggshells until Mum collapsed back into her bed. My favourite time was when Dad took me to work with him, when Aunty would sit with Mum. Early in the morning I would sit on Dad's bike handlebars and we would ride so fast the wind would whip my hair back off my face, and we would laugh at the people walking or bussing to work. I loved the feeling of freedom.

I would sit quietly in the depot and watch Dad carefully choose the colours to be mixed for the print run. I loved the smell of ink, watching the paper and magazines fly off the conveyer belt to be stacked into piles for the delivery trucks to roll in to pick them up. The drivers knew me by name, often teasing and sharing their morning tea with me. So, there was some reprieve. On the ride home we were both silent; who knew what condition Mum would be in?

Then Mum met a Dutch sailor, Otto; an aunty had bought him home to meet Dad, to do some odd jobs around the house. It was Otto who listened to her, wooed her, and gave her gifts. Mum cherished her Otto. In every sentence his name was mentioned, she then welcomed him as a boarder in our home and I became involved in their secrets. Notes were written and given to me to pass to Otto and vice versa. I would have been seven by then, still none the wiser about life, but the feeling I got was that this did not bode well at all.

Mum and Otto ran away. Our cases were packed, yes, I went as well. I still see the white note sitting on our kitchen table telling Dad we were leaving to live in Auckland, and my little heart was torn in two. I loved them both. We drove all night to Auckland city, stopping on the way at a fish and chip shop for dinner. Otto spoiled me with a chocolate ice cream. He booked us into a hotel, I was bathed and tucked up into a small trundle bed. My last question to Mum before I went to sleep was to ask when my dad was coming.

In the wee hours of the morning I woke to Mum and Otto having a huge row. He stormed out; Mum sobbed the hours away till daylight. Then she got up and said, 'Enough is enough,' then washed and dressed. Our train tickets were bought back to Wellington.

I have no idea what happened when Dad picked us up at the station. All I remembered is that Mum found herself a new church, with new friends who became her shoulder, her salvation. Bible meetings became a social outlet for her, the elders saying all was forgiven by God for any sins.

But I'm not like my Mum, am I?

It came to a time when I needed to admit to myself that yes, I was fast becoming antisocial. My hormones caused fluctuating bleeding. I had many escapes as I could feel the period begin with a severe cramp in the lower tum. There had been a couple of times I had not heeded the warning of nausea or cramps; I had even been caught out once on public transport going home from work. The family doctor said, 'You should carry more sanitary things with you.' Little did he know my work satchel contained so much sanitary gear I could not fit another tampon in. I switched to a female doctor after that day, the dread of becoming my mother lurked deeply inside my heart. The next time was the worst, it was during a work social. My husband's employer had shouted ten of the team to see the musical *Cats*. We were both delighted to accept; dinner and a show were not that often on our to-do list. It was a dress up occasion, which I loved. I was greeted with a wrist corsage by the big boss himself as we arrived.

We were shown to our seats and made sure we were all comfy. The lights went off, the curtain up, and the musical began. My heart soared with the music, only to feel that familiar cramp in my lower tum. Being in the middle of the row, I did not want to annoy others by leaving, so I talked myself into waiting for half time. That was, until another cramp; this one doubled me over. I knew I had to get out of the theatre, and fast. Too late, as I stood to exit, my period gushed, and I felt it flow down my legs and into my shoes. Thank God it was dark; I knew my beautiful black evening gown would be soaked. Making my way to the ladies' toilets, the attendant there saw my blood-soaked shoes, and rang for the First Aid lady to attend to me. An ambulance was called, and an announcement was made on stage for my husband to meet the medical team in the foyer immediately. I was cleaned up, given a hot sweet tea, and told that if it happened again I was to go straight to a hospital. This was serious.

The next day the doctor examined me and ordered scans to be taken, suggesting I take it easy for a day or two. 'You may have aborted a foetus,' she said.

I was stunned, 'I'm forty-five years old, Doc.'

She smiled, 'And stranger things have happened. I think we may look at a hysterectomy for you.'

When the day came for the operation, I just about ran to the theatre calling out, 'Don't start without me!'

Now without ovaries, womb, or uterus, surely any menopause symptoms would go away? How wrong I was. The aches and pains of my body were relentless, the tiredness that accompanied it, draining. My body now had a mind of its own. Plus, there were those fabulous mood swings; there were times I just wanted to shove a sock in my mouth (did I actually say that out loud?). My filter disappeared at social and family gatherings; any thought I had was blurted out in public.

To make matters worse, my emotions were always on high. If I heard a sad story or song my face would drip with tears. Or, if I heard something funny, sometimes the same reaction. This was not me. Invitations to events and family gatherings began dwindling. Our daughters asking me, 'Be careful what you say, Mum, please.'

So, I stayed away. Mum's saga crept into my mind; fear stood waiting to take my hand. I would mentally argue with myself, *but I'm not my mother, am I?*

I religiously practised positive thoughts, anything to turn my thoughts from dispatching a head or two with love and light. Life for me then was not a happy one. The medication, pills and creams my doctor had prescribed seemed to add to the feeling of slight vertigo and sadness, the headaches, the melancholy. My skin became papery and dry, lines formed around my mouth and I felt like I was a chameleon changing every day to suit my body's demands.

Hair now sprouted on my chin, my top lip was losing its youthful plumpness, and at my hairline a wide silver snake began to wind itself into my auburn hair. Sleep evaded me, and when I did finally fall sleep, nightmares of me turning into Mum.

Slowly, an unwanted muffin top was spreading around my waist. 'Why me? What the hell is this? Am I being punished for something I've done in my past? What's going on here? I can't do this anymore!' I sobbed in frustration in my doctor's rooms.

Her response was given with empathy, and sounding like she was scolding me as you would a child, said, 'It will soon be over, you're actually very healthy; all your bloods tests are excellent, try to exercise more and watch your diet, you're doing so well, hang on in there.' But, I wanted to know, when could I look forward to some peace from all this crap called menopause? When would it be over? There was no answer and I knew it, which made things worse.

No answer, at least, until one night, when sleep would not come; my husband lay there comatose, my two children the same, deep in the clutches of their dreams. Sleep was not happening, and in my sweaty, dripping desperation, I reached out online. I had seen a group starting up many months ago called, 'Menopause Madness'. I felt it was not right for me, but that night in desperation I found the website once more. I typed in my name; keen to chat to someone about my problems, answering the automatic question: was I female? I wanted to type an insult but thought better of it. No reply. I waited for a good five minutes, got myself a glass of water, settled back into the office chair to wait; it was better than tossing and turning in an overheated mess all night. If no-one answered in ten minutes, then an online card game would be the other option. As I waited, the water I sipped became tepid. 'Oh well, looks like it's a card game then,' I muttered to myself.

A line of words began to appear on the screen, *Hey Kez, it's Wanda here from Menopause Madness, good to see a new face, how are you?* Three hours later there were more than ten of us menopausal females chatting online. I felt so welcome, these ladies were amazing; herbal antidotes flowed, old-time remedies, modern-day pills and herbal potions, massage, aromatherapy: the list was long. There were some funny comments about husbands, families, and doctors, plus a lot of laughter between us. It felt like Mum's church group incarnate. Females helping females to understand, to hang on in there, reminding us we were doing this together. As the stories about menopause spilled out, I realised I was not alone. It was so helpful, some saying exercise and diet would help, others saying the less stress the better. Grab a quick snooze when you can, warm showers and lovely perfume, a decadent cocoa once a week. The main suggestion was to stay positive, to learn to live with it and, respect your body. For some, it was much worse than others. The main advice was that, as a band of women, we were strong. We were here for each other. Whenever someone reached out, another was there to listen, or, if I felt I could help another, I did. I felt uplifted, I had never thought about my advice as being of value to another woman, but why not?

I was thrilled that there was somewhere to go, someone to listen to me or that I could help another who also thought menopause sucked. Sleep was stealing over me when the alarm shattered my peace of mind. My husband was now up and in the shower. I could hear the kids stirring, soon it would be breakfast chaos, everyone wanting something before they went on their way to work and school. I announced I was not going into work today, my husband casually asked if I was not well; 'Another of your headaches?' He munched on his butter and jam laden toast while watching the morning news on telly.

'They're not MY headaches and I am well, I just don't feel like going to work, full stop.' Yes, I got that strange look of 'here we go again she's having another mood swing'. The kids yelled out their goodbyes, and I faced the kitchen bench full of dirty breakfast dishes. To hell with it, I'm having a PJ day, I stacked the dishwasher, wiped the bench down, threw the dish cloth into the washing machine. That was it for the day. I sauntered back to bed balancing a mug of hot tea and a plate of marmalade jam on toast. I plumped up my pillows, opened the windows to let in the sun and fresh air. Then, to keep a promise to myself, I took a slow walk on the beach, to the sun-kissed rock where the memories of a yesteryear had flooded in. I sat there savouring the fresh air, the sound of the waves encouraging me to leave the past behind, lifting my arms in the air I said, 'I am Me, Gloriously me!'

Gratefulness fills my heart, for today we have so much on offer to help us over our 'female problems' as they are called, that afternoon I went back to chatting with my new mates in Menopause Madness, the words of Wanda ringing in my head, and my new mantra.

'You are not alone; we are here to support you.'

Kez Wickham St George is a multi-inspired creative, dedicated to helping others bring out their voices, no matter their chosen creative platform. A bestselling multi-published author, poet and artist, Kez finds her passion in being a writers' consultant. She has created corridors between countries to entwine their creativities plus a radio host to raise the profile of authors and artists.

The greatest gift is to embrace who you are now and who you want to become in the future.

— Karen Mc Dermott

From My Heart to Your Heart

by Di Riddell

If only my younger self could have been blessed with the wisdom that I have accumulated over seven decades! But then, life doesn't work like that. It has been a journey with many detours and happenings that have shaped who I have become.

Today I sit in reflection. I think the seventh decade does that, or maybe I am allowing it. I live in love and gratitude for who I was, what was, and excitedly now, what is still to come. My life has stretched beyond all expectations, as I celebrate.

Two things have touched my heart recently. My fiftieth wedding anniversary is around the corner. It will not be celebrated, as my late husband is in heaven, yet his incredible, amazing, and loving effect on my life is ongoing.

And ... I am reflecting on the speech from Grace Tame, the Australian of the Year 2021. A survivor and advocate for child sexual abuse, Grace says, 'Survivors be proud, our voices are changing history.'

These words ring in my ears: 'There are still voices to be heard.' 'Every voice matters.' 'When we transform as individuals we transform as a community.' It starts with a conversation and we are all welcome at the table. You see, Grace lives in Tasmania where it was once against the law for a victim to speak out. Her abuser could speak out, and he did ... now, Grace can too.

I too am a survivor and thriver of sexual abuse. I lost my virginity to a pack rape at fifteen years of age. Back in the 1960s there was no support or consideration for girls. Abuse was considered to be her fault, she asked for it, she brought disgrace on her family. She was shamed and hidden away.

My mantra today is: your voice matters. My voice is necessary, and I express my truths with grace and power. Grace's five-minute speech expressed her truth with grace and power, and it touched me profoundly.

My own five-minute presentation has also touched many hearts ... It's all in the ad:

Wanted! A tall, dark and handsome man, fit and healthy, non-smoker, social drinker and a good sense of humour.

Sound good? What about this one?

Wanted! A crude, rude and rebellious man! A man who is only happy when making someone else feel they are stupid, useless and worthless?

Who would answer that ad? Any takers?
More to the point, who would place that ad?
I know someone who mentally placed that ad many times. She even got a reply. Come with me on a journey back to the 1960s with Marie.

Marie grew up in a violent, alcoholic household where confusion was the order of the day. She watched in fear as her mother was abused by her father and became conditioned to believe that this was how life was meant to be. Fear pervaded every aspect of her life.

Marie finally plucked up the courage to trust a boy. Nervous and excited, she agreed to meet him at a local dance. Afterwards he offered to drive her home and she innocently agreed. Marie hopped into the car and noticed, too late, that two mates were lying on the floor in the back of the car. They sped off into the night and took Marie to a deserted park where she was pack raped by the three men. Their hooting and hollering drowned out her pleas to stop, to take her home, to please, please stop.

Can you imagine Marie's fear, her terror, her revulsion? She was only fifteen.

Even more terrifying were the threats of what would happen if she told anyone. So she didn't, not even when she found she was pregnant as a result of the horrific incident.

The family packed her bags and sent her off to be berated by welfare workers. Her dad's ravings were nothing compared to those of the welfare workers. They said things like, 'Unclean, unworthy, loose morals, a disgrace to herself, her family and society.' 'Shame! Shame! Shame!' They screamed at her; 'No decent man will ever want you.'

Marie never got to see, touch, name or hear her baby. They made sure of that when they demanded she sign the adoption papers.

So, 'stupid, useless, unworthy and disgraceful' was how Marie was feeling when she placed the ad seeking someone rude and crude. After all, she thought, no decent man would want her.

Marie went on to fulfil her father's and the welfare workers' prophecies. Her descent into darkness was assured. She only associated with men who were drunk, abusive and violent. One night she saw her boyfriend's father hit his mother, knocking her across the room.

The woman turned to Marie and out of the corner of her mouth came the words Marie had always heard from her own mother, 'Well, I suppose I deserved that!' It was a turning point in Marie's life. The lightbulbs flashed wildly! She knew she had to get out of there. Get out! Get out now!

She gathered her courage and left, despite finding she was, once again, pregnant. Consider for a moment her anguish, her pain, her fear!

The welfare workers had a field day, Marie was now beyond redemption. A disgrace, she bought shame to all who knew her. Again, she was not allowed to see, hear, name or touch her baby – again it was taken from her and adopted out.

'Go and get a nursing job,' they said, 'where there is some discipline. And keep out of society's way!' So, she did.

Marie was kept under virtual lock and key; no leave passes were granted. They could do that because nurses lived in strictly controlled nursing quarters back then. She was watched and observed constantly. Marie saw nursing as her redemption, she worked hard and eventually built trust with Matron. After virtual house arrest, she was finally allowed to go out on a leave pass.

Marie accepted a blind date. Disbelief rang through the nurses' quarters as the news spread. Marie is going on a date! Fifteen girls lined up along the upper verandah of the old Queenslander peering through the railings of the nurses' quarters. Checking the appropriateness of any blind date was vital! Group approval was a huge component of the support system.

The car dove up and the Chinese whispers flew through the air: 'He looks normal.' 'Ooh, he has a suit on!' 'He looks safe.' Marie got the nod from the girls and off she went.

That date changed Marie's life. Hey, how do I know so much about Marie?

I am Marie. Marie is my middle name, the one that was hidden away. Like so many parts of my damaged life.

That blind date was with Les, my late husband. He was a gentle person and a gentleman. He saw me as the person with promise, not the one with the cruel negative labels I had been living with. He showed me real, unconditional love.

The devastating words that were tattooed on my brain from authority figures of my early life: 'stupid', 'useless' and 'worthless' were slowly erased with Les' gentle support.

The message here is that your past does not have to dictate your future. If any of you out there think that something you have done or experienced is so shameful, so horrible, that no one could ever love you, then think again.

I don't have all the answers, recovering from years of negativity takes time and work. To help me I have written a new ad.

It reads:

> *Wanted! One woman who has been to hell and back. One who deserves respect, who finds happiness and personal growth in other areas. A woman who can take a leap of faith and open up, overcome obstacles, and who believes in herself!*

I answer that ad every day.

Today, looking at it differently, I got to reflecting on what changed my way of thinking.

One incredible moment in time became the catalyst for my new life. I realised that a woman's total package goes way beyond anything I had ever dreamt. Beyond the physical, it stretches to embrace the emotional, spiritual, and shadow sides of her.

If I have learned one thing from my quietly confident self, it is to follow my heart. If something does not feel right then it probably isn't. As I struggled and resisted my new life as a widow, an avalanche of emotions left me wanting to hide, to run, to seek safety, when in fact the learnings were within me, waiting to be released – I just could not see them.

There I was, sitting with friends in the dappled sunlight on the veranda of a hospital room. It was 4 September 2002. The conversation flittered from subject to subject. We all knew why we were there. The warm and fuzzy feeling I was getting from supportive friends was shattered by an earth-shattering scream of, 'Dianne – come quick.'

Three paces took me to my husband's bedside and three minutes later he was gone. Three things hit me: I was alone, I was scared, and I did not want to accept it. The love of my life, the man who showed me unconditional love and the man who had adored me for thirty-one years lay lifeless before me.

Little did I know that this was to be a pivotal point, one that would lead to a changed outlook on my life, that it would help me to release the shackles of my past and allow me to make a difference in the lives of other women.

How I would love to say that I picked up, pushed on and positivity shone from every pore. No, no, no! It was, however, time for me to be catapulted into the life of a widow. How that term grated on me as I groped and clawed my way forward! Today, looking back, I scarcely recognise that woman.

My coping mechanism was to work harder, faster, and longer than I ever had before. I was totally involved in anything and everything. I cleaned and fussed and pushed, pushed, and pushed harder. I have never liked eating alone - so I stopped. It was not a conscious decision to lose weight, it just seemed somehow natural to my confused brain.

Twelve kilograms fell from an already tall, slim frame. One morning I just could not do anything, my body had come to a screaming halt and I knew I needed help. The flurry began with doctors and psychologists; my self-help journey began and gradually gained momentum.

It was a huge challenge for me to take that first step. Dealing with my grief sent me back to face those significant early childhood challenges when mental abuse was the order of the day, and physical violence was directed at my mother, with the implication that I was next. I had spent a lonely, frightened, and unhappy childhood. I saw myself as a young teenager with no self-confidence, no self-esteem and no self-belief leading into the rape, pregnancy, and adoption of my babies.

With Les I created an amazing, fun filled, challenging life … suddenly it was all gone.

The main things that supported me through that time were acknowledging and accepting that I was responsible for my own life and what happens to me. Life is meant to be enjoyed and filled with health, vitality, and confidence.

At my lowest point, I began journaling. It was a deep journey of healing: the kind where all my walls came down and I was faced with the raw emotion and truth of who I was and how I felt about life. Along with my husband, I had lost my identity.

It wasn't easy. I was facing my own vulnerabilities and a pile of negatives you could not jump over. I was seeking, seeking, to let go, to see myself in a new light and move forward. Who can Di Riddell be in this world? What is possible for her?

My heart took me to great places, and I began to accept and understand that love conquers all, starting with self-love.

I developed and honed my confidence and my resilience by continually embracing, and often resisting, the changes in my new life, seeking joy, happiness and enjoyment in the simple things that made me smile. Journaling every day constantly re-programmed my mind for what I wanted to bring into my life, and from that place I attracted and received. Learning and practicing techniques and processes that I use to this day helped me to continue to grow as a person. A real biggie; I learned to be kind to myself.

Embracing forgiveness and gratitude was heart healing. Part of my journey was writing and self-publishing my story, *Beyond Abuse*.

In order to be able to write that book I needed to come to a point of forgiveness and show gratitude to Dad and the rapists. I could never have written it otherwise. That message flowed through me then, as it does now and continues into my future.

Becoming an author evolved; you could even call it accidental. My background was nursing and that job description did not include writing creatively. Toastmasters' five-to-seven-minute speeches hardly predisposed me to serious writing. Yet reading has always been a passion. Reading took me to places I had not contemplated – it allowed me to live vicariously through others' stories. Words and books give me the power to ignite my imagination, to help and see the world through perspectives other than my damaged one, and leave me in awe and wonder at the marvels of the human spirit.

I learned to love the characters, to live their life and put myself in the 'for instance'. There were serious challenges along the way that dented my confidence. Coping, handling things I had never had to handle before. My perceived shortcomings I saw as failures, as burdens, and they weighed me down.

Still journaling, I took a serious move into everything to do with self-development – took hold of me and took on a life of its own. In 2018 I re-released *Beyond Abuse: a recovery guide for men and women in an era of me, and all of us, too*. The day I received the link, lights flashed and exploded in my mind and I thought, I am ready … it's time. My author journey opened me to search for the two children I had adopted out.

What a roller-coaster ride it was. In two short months I had found, met, and hugged my daughter who lives in another suburb of my city, the daughter I never thought I would see, hear, or touch. Can you imagine the myriad of emotions that flooded through me? Joy, happiness, fear, shivers, exhilaration, rejection, empathy, compassion, and hope – to name a few.

I wanted to do something special. I wanted my daughter Sue to receive something personal from me along with her paperwork, prior to our meeting, to start a conversation of silver threads to connect us.

My choice was to write a letter, a very personal letter. Sharing what I thought she would want to know, my secrets revealed, because family secrets hidden away can fester for decades, sometimes generations. It was my choice to break the cycle as I believe that speaking up and sharing is vital to the healing process.

In keeping quiet, silence howls in the background, creating internal havoc. Silence leads to powerlessness, and together they are a deadly combination that keep us in pain, and in the shadows.

> *Dear Sue,*
> *It is like a dream come true, exciting, exhilarating, yet scary. On one hand we have no shared history, on the other we are connected through the process of birth.*
> *It is not my intention to disrupt your life, I will respect your privacy by giving you all the space you need. You will also want to move at your own pace, processing your thoughts.*
> *The circumstances surrounding your adoption were outside of my control, my basic rights were denied me throughout the process. That included not being allowed to see you, to touch you, or to give you a name. You were whisked away from me at the moment of birth with no discussion being entered into. Adoption affects so many, it reaches way beyond the mum and the baby.*
> *You have stayed in my thoughts over the years, I told myself that*

I would not search but my arms would be open if you reached out to me. Then I changed my mind. My consolation was that a couple who had wanted you would be able to care for and support you in a way that I could not.

It is with heartfelt gratitude that I learned that you have been happy and have wonderful adoptive parents, as was promised to me by the people who had the power over your adoption.

Life was vastly different in the 1960s. Society's attitudes were far more insensitive and rigid. The reasons I had never reached out include that I was protecting my own mum, and felt if you had had a happy life, I did not want to disrupt it. This had a huge impact on me. My life was sad and unhappy for a long time.

The only way for me to cope when you were taken from me was to disconnect. There was no help available back then. I had to disconnect to survive. I could not grieve or share my thoughts and emotions. I was locked in silence and shame. Now I have had decades of deep self-development, waiting, exploring, writing and now the unbelievable has happened, here you are, my daughter! I have this amazing God-given opportunity to meet you.

You are now a mature woman. I wonder about your life path. Are you as curious as I am about your eye colour, how tall you are, and your interests? Are you a left-hander? Do you dislike bananas? So many questions; where do I start?

It is important to me that I share that I am a published author, having shared my story with the world.

With love and kindness, Di

I asked myself, Is this possible? Is it really going to happen? I had to pinch myself, then contain my excitement when I was notified that Sue would be delighted to meet me …

It happened; we met, and it was wonderful. It was an experience that touched my soul, it was almost too fantastic to describe. And it all began with taking the first step of reaching out.

On that beautiful morning I took along a gift of a miniature rose to celebrate new beginnings and a card for her adoptive mum (the only mum she had known), thanking her for giving Sue the life that I couldn't. Tears of happiness flowed when we met, I opened my arms and she walked right into them, hugged, stepped back and looked into each other's eyes, basking in that electrifying moment.

Looking beyond the personal into my current world of writing, speaking and coaching, nothing gives me greater pleasure than seeing a woman step confidently into her power. Today I am a richer and more compassionate woman. I chose to connect and work with mature women. I believe that when we face significant life challenges others need a hand, just like I did.

My third book is *Speak Out: from suppression to expression in 9 vital steps to know that your voice matters.* It is a unique blend of storytelling, strategies, and action steps. It is an elixir for all kinds of emotional ailments and guides you to connect with the knowing that you are worth it. Knowing that your voice matters enables you to engage and upgrade your thinking and move forward.

We have the opportunity to look to the next generation, to our daughters and granddaughters. Let's teach them that their voice is a tool to be valued, what they have to say is important and needs to be heard. Let's also teach them to speak with grace and power, to create love, light, and laughter in their voices, to leave the table when respect is no longer being served, to be silly, brave, and strong, to be confident, authentic, and real.

Our voices matter, every one of them, and they are necessary for us all to express our truths with grace and power. A woman who heals herself heals her mother, heals her daughter and every woman around her. A favourite saying of mine is …

A helping hand does not stop at the wrist it extends all the way to the heart – from my heart to your heart.

And a lovely man has answered my advert and is now in my life.

My passion is confidence - that extraordinary energy in you that is attractive, strong, vibrant, and engaging. You know it when you see it ... and say, 'I want some of what she's got.'

Those words carried me over many a challenge and I share them from my sacred heart space.

Di Riddell is the voice, catalyst and game changer for women who have had their voices suppressed. She describes herself firstly as a woman, mentor, lover and friend; roles that have brought love, joy, and happiness on many levels.

Secondly, she is a writer, published author, NLP practitioner, speaker, and home beautifier, all of which provide stimulation.

Finally, Di is a business owner and coach. As a heart-driven woman, Di is dedicated to helping others to use their confident voice in order to be the person they most want to be.

www.diriddell.com

How I Learned to Love My Shadow

by Amanda Schubert

I don't remember exactly how or when she was created. But I remember the first thing she told me:

You aren't good enough.

She existed as a voice in my mind, an echo that whispered to me in my darkest moments; those times when my self-belief was wavering. She was my shadow.

No-one will ever like you.
You're too different.
Why are you even trying?

My story is not about how I defeated her, or even silenced her. It is about how I learned to love her.

I was a quiet child. Not necessarily shy, but I tended toward introversion rather than extroversion. 'Conscientious' was a common word in all of my primary school reports; Amanda is a conscientious student. I never really understood what that meant back then. I enjoyed learning and loved being creative, qualities that have not diminished over time. But one aspect of my early school days has shaped me far more than I gave it credit for at the time.

You see, it was through my peers that I learned that I would never fit in.

One of my earliest memories was starting my first year as a reception, coming into a class that already had students who had bonded and formed friendships. The other incoming students and I had to stand in front of the class and select which child we wished to be our class buddy, to help us settle in and feel welcomed. I spotted a friendly-looking girl who had already taken one of us newbies under her wing. I pointed her out to the teacher, but before I could say a word, she widened her eyes and shook her head rapidly, frowning at me. It was my first taste of rejection, and it stung. She ended up with two more buddies. But I was not chosen. I was not good enough.

Over the years, I began to realise that I was not like the others. I was not the pretty one, or the smart one, or the sporty one, or the wealthy one. Little cliques formed around me, groups of kids who had things in common, who had found their matches. I stayed on the outside, never quite finding a place – and I began to hear her for the first time. My shadow. The one who whispered to me that I was not enough. Not pretty enough. Not smart enough. Not sporty enough. Not rich enough.

So, I did the only thing my young heart knew to do – I made the pain go away. I shoved it deep inside, pushing into the darkness where it couldn't hurt me. I didn't realise it then, but I was only feeding the shadow, making it stronger. By giving it what it craved – my insecurity, my misery, my self-doubt – I allowed it to grow.

'You have to hide. It's the only way to stay safe. Trust me. Don't speak to them because they'll laugh at you. Don't draw attention in class because they will whisper about you behind your back. Don't do anything that will let them know how different you are – hide, little one. Stay safe.'

Hiding was easy. I kept my hair long and never wore it up; it became my shield. I never raised my hand in class, even when I knew the answer, and never spoke unless I was forced to. At playtime, I found the quietest corner of the playground and sheltered amongst the trees and bushes. Against the odds, I found two friends, two boys who were like me. The first glimmer of hope emerged – perhaps I wasn't so different after all. But that flickering candlelight did little to diminish the power of the shadow. She was just getting started.

By the time I reached puberty, I was struggling immensely with bullying. I've always been a larger girl, and despite my desire to hide away, this drew the nastiness to me like moths to a flame. I stopped eating at school. I gave my food away to my friends and made sure no-one ever saw me eating. Lunchtimes brought with them a whole new level of fear. I began to dread them, wishing we could stay in the classroom with teacher supervision for the whole day. At least then I would have some protection from the barbed comments and the laughs at my expense. This, I realised later, was my first dance with my shadow's new friend – anxiety.

My anxiety fuelled my shadow and it relished in it. By the time I reached my final primary school years, I was wearing jumpers and long-sleeved shirts all year round, even when the mercury hit the high thirties. Baggy pants, baggy jumpers, and my long hair hiding my face became the norm. As if I wasn't already struggling enough in my battle to retain some semblance of self-worth, I developed terrible acne and required braces for my teeth. It was like the universe was giving my bullies their every desire, every imperfection they needed for their weapons.

Despite it all, there was still that spark in me, that flicker of hope in the darkness. My loyal friends, the boys, had never wavered in their love for me, in their friendship. Years later, one of them would remark to me that one of his greatest memories was watching me play with bees on the school oval. It was true; I would spend my lunchtimes searching the lawn for wayward bees, collecting them on little plastic lids or leaves, and transporting them to a safer place. No matter how much I was hurting and struggling, I never lost my kindness and compassion. I didn't realise then how important that would be; that inner light that never dimmed.

High school was kinder to me. Well, on the outside, at least. Whether maturity played a role, or perhaps my skin had just grown thicker, it is hard to tell. But the bullying seemed to fade away. My circle of friends had expanded, and I was rediscovering how it felt to bond with people, to share in the security that comes with having a companion to experience the waves of life with. My shadow, however, had grown exponentially.

I still felt insecure amongst my peers, though it had evolved into more of a sense of apathy; I had no interest in trying to be their friend, but I still wanted them to like me. So, I kept up my defences and shields, staying quiet and not drawing attention to myself. I had developed this perception that I was 'blending in', and if not being liked by them, I was at least accepted. Until one particular day that I remember in vivid detail.

My anxiety was rife by now. Some days, it was all I could muster just to get out of bed. I still struggled with eating in front of people, of having eyes on me, and giving a class presentation made me feel nauseous and faint. I had been given the task of writing an essay on the gold rush and presenting it to my class. My anxiety overwhelmed me and I hadn't done it. I expected there to be consequences; after all, I hadn't done my homework. But my teacher decided to do something I wasn't expecting. And it was the worst possible thing that could have happened at that point in my life; she made me stand up in front of the whole class and justify to them why I didn't do the assignment. Then, they would decide whether I should go free or if I deserved to be punished.

That moment – the moment when I, at fourteen, had to stand before my peers as they unanimously decided that I didn't deserve to get away with it and shouted reasons why my excuse (that I had felt 'sick' – I didn't understand then that it had been a panic attack) was not good enough – solidified my shadow and gave her all the fuel she needed to completely overtake me.

See? You see now how worthless you are? They don't care about you, they never will. Because you are not good enough – you will never be good enough.

I stopped caring after that day. If I was never going to be 'good enough', what was the point of it all? My grades dropped. I stopped playing sport. I squashed all my feelings deep down into the darkness and learned how to be witty and sarcastic, honing my skills of deflection and distraction so no-one could see the 'real me', only the mask that I wanted them to see. I hardened my demeanour and hid myself away behind a wall of 'I don't give a shit'.

Depression and anxiety became my normal. When it came time to start thinking about my career after high school, I had nothing. I wasn't interested in anything anymore, not least getting a job. All I wanted to do was hang out with my friends and just keep coasting on. My passion was gone, swallowed by the shadow, and I had no long-term goals or interests. On the outside, I portrayed this under the guise of carefree confidence. On the inside, I was hollow and empty.

I owe my life to the friends I had back then. The words 'find your tribe' are thrown around a lot these days, but they perfectly sum up the people I had around me during what I would later come to realise was my darkest hour. These friends, they saw me. Not the mask, not the sharp-tongued girl with the quick wit and nippy comebacks, or even the tough girl that didn't care what people thought. They saw beneath all that – the vulnerable me who craved acceptance and approval, and who, above all, just wanted to be loved for who she was. And they did love me. It was what kept me going when I believed I couldn't. My tribe. My soul companions.

Over the course of the next decade my life changed dramatically. I met and married my husband and started a family at a young age. Our first child was a daughter, and it fuelled a quite different part of me – that flickering light, that spark that had stood against everything the darkness had thrown at it, burst into flame. I knew then that I had to heal, I had to face my shadow so that I could be the best mother to her I could. My intentions were good, my motivation unquestionable …

But my methods were flawed.

You see, my shadow had become so intertwined with my soul that I couldn't separate them. My shadow told me the reason I had to heal was because I was broken – that I could not be a good mother unless I was perfect. Failure, it reasoned, was not an option. To be anything less than the best was to let her down – my beautiful daughter. I would do everything I could to be perfect for her.

I was extremely hard on myself, then. When things went wrong, I berated and punished myself for not being – you guessed it – good enough. My daughter struggled with breastfeeding and sleeping – it must be my fault. I was emotional and overwhelmed – it's because I'm not strong enough. Depression consumed me, and I reverted to my tried and true coping methods; hide away, don't let anyone see how much you're struggling, and never let the mask fall.

My old insecurities were flooding back with abundance. All those memories I had shoved deep down inside me were being gleefully thrown in my face by my shadow, reminding me of all the times I had failed. Motherhood, I learned, can overwhelm you with a tidal wave of comparisons if you aren't prepared.

And I hadn't packed my life jacket.

The other mums are better than you. Their babies sleep more. They can breastfeed, you couldn't. They had natural births – you had to have a C-section because you failed at going into labour. Look at you – you gained even more weight while they all got skinny. You'll never be a good mum.

The birth of my son a few years later came with even more struggles. But I never faltered in my love for them. Quite the opposite, in fact. My capacity for love had always been high – but I would pour it into others and leave nothing for myself. Self-sacrificing was a large part of my identity, and I felt the high of self-worth when I made others happy. But I see now that it was just an echo. What I believed to be self-worth was, in reality, my kindness and compassion for others. Not that they were bad, of course; I just didn't understand that they are not the same thing.

Around the time my daughter started school, a lot of my old anxieties came up. I worried endlessly that she would be bullied, that the other children would be cruel or exclude her – that she would feel the same rejection that I'd felt. It was worse when my son started, as he had some developmental delays, and I could hardly sleep from the panic that he would be made to feel any less than the beautiful soul he is. They were the mirror I needed to finally see the shadow I'd been avoiding for so long. Through my love for them and my desire for their happiness, I was forced to face my own fears and doubts.

But healing is not always beautiful. It can be messy and painful and raw. I had spent decades fighting my emotions, refusing to feel them, and storing anything painful deep inside where it couldn't hurt me. My masks, the personas I had developed so carefully, had kept me safe from others. If I lost that, if they saw the real me, I could be rejected again. I could be laughed at, or belittled, or reminded that I am not like them and I don't belong – I never will. No, it was best to just keep going like I had been. Hide away. Blend in. Don't draw attention. That is what would keep me safe.

The final push I needed to finally confront my shadow came with the loss of one of my dearest friends. At the age of only twenty-eight he was diagnosed with cancer. This was the same friend who had reminded me of the girl he had always seen – the one who played with bees on the school oval. Before he passed, my other friend and I went to visit him. Just the three of us, the same trio who had been together from the very beginning; just me and the two boys who had known me back before I had put on any of my masks.

He told me then how much he had always believed in me. That he had always known I was capable of more than I believed. We reminisced about the times before; before the darkness, before I lost who I was, before I decided to hide myself away and give up on my dreams. The greatest gift he ever gave me was the gift of being seen. Despite everything I had done to lock my soul away, he had loved me exactly for who I was. Even now, I still know he is around, watching over and guiding me, reminding me to never forget who I am.

I knew it was time to heal, then. To truly heal. Not for my family, not for my friends, but for me. For the little girl with the bees. For the girl who had shown so much love and kindness to others while neglecting herself. And for the shadow, who had been hurting for such a long, long time. It wouldn't happen quickly; things that important rarely do. But I wanted to start.

The first step was realising how much of my pain had been self-inflicted. If I put the list of all the hurtful comments I'd received over the years side by side, it would soon become obvious that I had belittled, ridiculed and demoralised myself far more than anyone else. That voice in my head, the one I called my shadow, was my greatest source of pain. Until I learned to forgive her, and to treat her with kindness, I would always be my own worst enemy.

You see, in truth, my shadow has always loved me. All those times she told me to hide away, to not show myself, she was trying to keep me safe. But she didn't know how. My masks were created to protect my precious soul from pain, the darkness brought to hide my light where no-one could extinguish it. To free it, I had to convince my shadow that we would be okay. Because she is a part of me, too. Fighting her would not fix anything. I had to show her that it was safe, that hiding from the world was not the way to live. She was my inner child, and all she had ever wanted was love.

Healing is not always straightforward. My life has not suddenly changed to one where I am positive and smiling and dancing-in-the-street happy every single day. I get overwhelmed. I have days where I can't face the thought of seeing people and cannot muster the strength to even go to the supermarket. I feel a sense of panic every time someone comes to the door when I'm not expecting visitors. Eating in public is still a trial. Calling someone on the phone is an ordeal and I'll often put off returning a call for days.

Feeling 'good enough' is still difficult. I am harsh on myself when I believe that I have 'failed'. I get panic attacks and sensory overload in crowded places and still feel the twisty feeling in my stomach around others when I worry what they are thinking of me, if they are judging me. I still wear a lot of masks, though they are less about shielding myself now and more about helping me to feel confident when I am afraid. My shadow is still learning to let go and not hold onto grudges anymore.

But there has been a lot of joy, too. More than I could have imagined back in those younger days. I am taking risks now, putting myself out there and grabbing opportunities with both hands. I'm now a published author, a dream I have clung to for as long as I can remember. I have found several 'tribes'; groups of friends where I am embraced for exactly who I am and loved fiercely for being me. I have made connections across the globe and fulfilled my dream of travelling to Ireland. If you had told teenage me that I would have the confidence to travel to the other side of the world all by myself to not only meet with a group of strangers but give a speech to them, I never would have believed you. But I did. And it has changed my life in more ways than I can count.

If I could describe my life these days in one word, I would say I am content. It's not perfect, and I would never claim to have the ideal life! But my heart feels clear. I can recognise when my shadow is trying to protect me, and I thank her for it. I also know when I need to step out into the light and allow myself to be seen and can do that with greater confidence than ever before. With this new clarity and sense of self, I am also finding freedom in helping my children navigate their own shadows. I see them, and I make sure they know they are seen for the precious, unique souls they are.

My colours are a kaleidoscope of lights and darks, of hope and shadow. I have many aspects, many stories, many experiences that have shaped me and will continue to grow as my life unfolds. I have loved and lost and experienced exhilaration and heartache. There will always be times when I find myself wallowing in the darkness, but I know that the sun will come out again. I no longer feel shame or regret about my choices or wish that things had gone differently. I have forgiven myself and others for the mistakes. I am who I am today because of them; because of all the souls I have walked this journey with – the ones who hurt me, and the ones who loved me. Because of the moments that I have lived, of the good and the bad.

These are *The Colours of Me*. And they are truly beautiful.

Amanda Schubert was born and raised in the Riverland region of South Australia. She's a mother, YA fantasy author, children's book illustrator, and school librarian. In 2019, she travelled to Ireland for a writers' retreat at Crom Castle, where she made her debut as an international speaker. This was the moment that led to her achieving her dream of publishing her first novel, *'The Bards of Birchtree Hall'*, and she hasn't looked back.

When she isn't writing, Amanda enjoys spending her time reading, drawing, and creating memories with her husband and two children.

Being deeply loved by someone gives you strength, while loving someone deeply gives you courage.

— Lao Tzu

Are you Listening Now?

by Danielle Aitken

It is an interesting concept to think of life as a series of events that add vibrant colour to the recipient's palette, however this is exactly what I know to be true about life. For me, this is a truth as inevitable as when the tiny trickle of alpine water flows forth to eventually become the great river – it will carve a path as it diverts around immovable obstacles and shapes the surrounding landscape on its mighty journey to the ocean. You and I are a lot like the river; we grow emotionally in strength and wisdom from the experiences of our lifetime as we travel along the stream of life's events. When we choose to open our hearts and minds to the lessons provided, we navigate our path from the source to the eventual destination on this exhilarating journey we call life. If we are wise, we learn to bend, yield, and divert just like the mighty river, collecting colourful pebbles along the way, in the form of precious wisdom from life's encounters; experiences that add colour and texture to the beautiful tapestry that becomes our bigger picture.

I have learned so much along my way, as has every one of you I'm sure; so many valuable lessons, so much precious wisdom, but I am well aware that I am still a work in progress with so much more to learn. For me, learning is an invaluable gift that I intend to continue to receive until the day I die.

When I sat to write this chapter, I was challenged to choose exactly what it was I wanted to speak about. That single episode that has shaped me the most, but you see there is no single episode because life is a journey of learnings, and so, as I feel the words beginning to form and flow with my intention to write something of value, I surrender to this process and begin to write intuitively. This is how I choose to live my life. Thus, I am open to receive and the words that keep coming to me at this moment are 'trust', 'knowing', and 'are you listening?' Particularly the latter. This has proven to be my universal mantra, a wake-up call of sorts, you see once, not so very long ago, I was not listening. I was not listening to my body and I was ignoring my own needs, as many 'healers', 'helpers' and mothers often do. Due to this, I was struck down by an autoimmune disease that completely took my legs out from under me, metaphorically and in every other way. I was not like the mighty river, not diverting, not going with the flow, no – I was swimming upstream, against the tide – full steam ahead in my own direction. No time for self-care, no time to rest.

To explain, I need to go back into the past, to see where the seeds were sown for the eventual catastrophic crash that was awaiting me. Why? You see, the magnificence of the body that guides us through this life is extraordinarily resilient. It can and will do its utmost to keep functioning and compensating until it can compensate no more. It has become very apparent to me over my own journey, that the body desires to be healthy. It will give you certain warning signs when things are not going well. Signs that, when heeded, may divert the flow of the mighty torrent of things to come so that it is possible to paddle to the safety of a sheltered haven by taking effective action, in doing so preventing the impending calamity of going headfirst into the damaging rapids. These crucial signs may be something akin to a quiet 'tap on the shoulder'.

... Hello? Are you listening? ... No ... Really?

Perhaps you should!
The ever-resilient body may send many such warning signs, as it did for me.
Another tap on the shoulder ... another whisper ... *Are you listening yet?*
I was a busy mother, working full time in a high-pressure job, attending to the needs of all; except for myself.
I had been struggling with an undiagnosed inflammatory condition since I was eighteen years old.
Even at this young age, I now know that I had been metaphorically carrying a heavy burden on my shoulders. After ten years of extremely painful inflammation, and life-affecting limitations with no apparent diagnosis, laxity of ligaments was finally offered up by the surgeon who was prepared to take me on. Multidirectional joint instability ...
'No wonder you are in so much pain!'
At last, I thought ... someone finally understands what is happening to me. I left the consulting rooms that day, got to my car and cried out of sheer and utter relief.
Four operations later, mostly failed, followed by ridiculous amounts of physiotherapy, hydrotherapy, acupuncture, and every other kind of therapy you could imagine, I was eventually left to manage on my own as best I could. A deafening question was being asked by my body, but I could not hear it.

Are You Listening Now?

Are you listening yet?

During this challenging time, I even sought a second opinion from a clinician who was 'top of his game', reportedly 'the best in his field', only to be told by this 'specialist' at the tender age of twenty-nine ... and I quote ...

'I'm sorry, there is nothing that can be done for you. You are going to be in pain for the rest of your life!'

This time I did not make it to my car to cry. I had pinned my hopes on this 'medical expert'. Tears of distress began to flow upon hearing those prejudicial words, even before I left the consulting room, despite the fact I did my utmost to withhold them as I defiantly did not want to give him the satisfaction of seeing my distress. By the time I made my way to the reception desk to pay for the privilege of being sentenced to a life of pain, I was blinded by tears and unable to speak. Later, those tears of distress turned to anger as I became outraged at this man's lack of integrity in spending less than six minutes in total with me only to slap me with a life sentence. *How dare he!* I fiercely thought.

Nothing ever stays the same, this is true, and my condition began to worsen and morph into something more. Still with no diagnosis, I was victim to the sudden nature of its onset. All the while I did my best to manage my career and a young family with the limitations of my physical restrictions. There were many lessons to be learned during this time. One of the major ones was for the first time in my life I had to learn to ask for help. It did not come easily for me; I had always been the 'helper'. Naturally, people rushed to assist. This affliction now affected other joints, usually only one at a time. A knee, then a hip, occasionally a wrist, each for months at a time and still nobody had any answers for me as to why this was happening.

I now recognise these as my warning signs, my 'listen up' opportunities. but none of this prepared me for what was to come.

My body was constantly trying to get my attention in the only way it knew how. It was, in fact, asking me the question over and over again.

Hello? ... Are you listening?

I was not.

For a time, I settled into my life with this affliction. Sometimes I felt sorry for myself, although generally not for long. As a registered nurse I was well aware that there were many people far worse off than me, and I reminded myself of this whenever I needed a little shove out of self-pity.

I'm not sure exactly when I began to search for answers that were not to be found in Western medicine. It was probably during my latter years of working in IVF when I was desperately trying to arm myself with more tools to assist those struggling with the difficult infertility journey. Already a registered nurse and midwife with considerable experience, I set my intention and became a counsellor. This was a turning point for me personally, as I began to discover the amazing power and potential of our mind to create change simply by challenging and changing our thoughts. This was my catalyst to learn more, and learn more I did. I was like a sponge taking it all in. I once again furthered my education at that point by becoming a clinical hypnotherapist. Now things began to get really interesting, as I continued to delve into the principals of mind-body potential, neuroplasticity, epigenetics, and quantum physics. The resounding message was that the body knows how to heal itself and meditation, hypnosis, energy work and absolute belief were the keys to unlock this potential. Mind over matter – I was discovering that where the mind goes, the body follows.

Paper after paper, book after book based on well-formulated, evidence-based research showed beyond a shadow of doubt, that every single thought we have instantly produces chemical and physical responses in our bodies directly related to those thoughts. This was empowering. I was inspired.

I started to practice the principles of mind-body medicine and the more I did, the more I began to see marked improvements in my physical and emotional health.

I was healing my body.

In 2017, however, despite having become skilled at seeing potential warning signs, a disastrous crash was impending. Sent to teach me more, as my body emphatically stated once again in the only way it could – enough was enough. When we choose to ignore the warning whispers, the deafening roar that begs the question again; *Are you listening?* … often inevitably follows. I liken this to be something akin to the mighty river bursting its banks as the seemingly futile dam wall that has sought to restrain the powerful torrent eventually gives way.

My dam wall, which had stemmed the progress of my inflammatory condition, gave way in spectacular fashion after I had broken my lower left leg two weeks before a much-anticipated three-day Hay House writers workshop in Sydney, Australia. For me, this event had signalled the beginning of my writing journey. An important milestone: the falling of the chequered flag signalling the journey was beginning. Missing it was NOT an option. So, with moon boot in position, airport wheelchair arranged, hobbling on crutches completely unable to weight bear, I drove myself to the airport with only what I could carry on my back.

My husband was not a fan of this choice; nonetheless, off I went. As you may imagine, many of the challenges had been unforeseen. Not least of all was the final, seemingly never-ending journey at 10 pm across the long-term car park at Tullamarine airport. The crowded airport bus was filled with noisy return travellers who clearly could not see that just south of my exhausted expression, I was desperately trying to protect a broken leg from bumps and knocks. I disembarked one stop early, deciding this was a better option and 'crutched it' to my waiting car. 'It's not far,' I told myself.

As I reflect on that trip to Sydney there are a couple of things that stand out in my mind. Some are writing 'gems', but the one thing that stands out the most are those last few 'crutch-assisted' steps to my car. I had to will myself to keep going with a mantra playing in my head with each exhausted step … 'Nearly there.' I arrived at my car almost too exhausted to open the door and collapsed into the seat totally spent, crying in utter relief and exhaustion, 'Thank God. I made it!'

Still defiantly pleased I had gone but knowing it had been a step way too far; I was very aware that my body was not happy. The subsequent inflammation I experienced was like nothing I had experienced before. Almost every joint in my body was impacted. Both feet, knees, hips, back, wrists, fingers and even my jaw was affected such that I couldn't chew or bite.

… Are you listening now?

Yes, God! I was listening. I threw myself into my healing: meditating daily, minding my thoughts, and choosing very carefully what to focus on and what to let slip into the background without judgement. There was so much I could not do at the time, but I could not focus on that. I had to focus on what I could do, what I did have and what was working. It was at this time of not even being able to hold a pen to write, that I began to tap out a story of resilience and hope on my laptop with the fingers that were able to do so.

Out of my adversity came an opportunity and *Sarah's Story: Life After IVF,* the book that had been waiting to be written, was born.

I remain incredibly grateful for the opportunity.

Life continues for me in predictable ways now. My self-care practices are my daily non-negotiables, however, it is always possible to unwittingly slip back to old patterns and habits, as I was about to learn.

26 December 2020

I was awoken at 2:34 am by a searing pain in my right foot that took my breath away. Unable to walk, I was assisted to the bathroom by my ever-attentive husband, as the thought, *this cannot happen again,* immediately came to mind, accompanied by an 'Oh God, not today' dread. I had already hosted a large family, traditional Christmas lunch the day before, and Boxing Day was to be another. I had house guests and family for lunch and no time for this! I immediately sprang into action, well actually, my husband did because I could not, as he quickly gathered everything I requested. An icepack from the freezer, compression bandaging and a rather large dose of Prednisolone, a medication I had not needed for over eighteen months!

At that moment, my trust and belief that my body knows how to heal itself was in direct conflict with the other absolute knowing: this inflammation was created by stress, of which I had experienced more than my share in the last two weeks. I put on my headphones and settled in for a lengthy meditation session.

Morning came and I could put my foot to the ground, but only just. I scooted about the kitchen that day on a rolling office chair, determined that I would not resort to the use of the wheelie walker I had retired many years ago, as I attempted to get through the day with as minimal movement as possible.

I know that we have the ability to heal our own bodies, I have done it before; I set my firm intention to do it again. The next day, against all odds, I could walk well enough to cautiously navigate the beach sand, so that I could immerse my body in the healing cool ocean waters of Kilcunda. It was just what I needed. The sea heals not only my body, but my soul. I had to wonder as I floated in the refreshing water looking at the sky, *why don't I come down here every day?* A small promise to do so, winter or summer, was made to myself, slightly before the reality of busy life crashed in to my musings. I then edited my intention so that it resembled something I may actually be able to achieve. With this in mind, the next day I again made my way across the sand, more easily this time, and again immersed my body in the cool ocean water for thirty minutes. This, combined with daily meditation, Tai Chi and carefully chosen footwear saw me miraculously healed and walking normally within three days. Fantastic!

Unfortunately, though I was about to get another lesson as the universal words of wisdom were about to sound in my ears again.

Are you listening yet?

What went wrong? I had been rushing about cleaning and preparing for two weeks of various guests that the Christmas week heralded, combined with shopping, and preparing for Christmas Day and Boxing Day functions, as I tried to finish up the year that was, with an overfilled client diary. I was also dealing with an unprecedented, particularly upsetting, client event combined with inevitable family dynamics and concerns. Two of my children were also attempting to navigate their own rough waters and wanted much needed support from their mum. What I didn't really acknowledge at the time was that I was sitting smack bang in the middle of a perfect storm of stressful events, and stressful energy similar to that which created my illness in the first place, all swirling about me like a whirling dervish. Naturally, I saw the warning signs, of course I did, but what could I do? It was Christmas.

1 January 2021: 5:30 am

I was awakened by a searing pain in my right foot, that took my breath away … Again.

Are you listening NOW?

I was completely unable to walk and could now feel the inflammation quickly spreading to other areas of my body.

YES! I am listening now, and thank you; I am grateful for the lesson learnt.

I have no excuse, none. The lesson this time is to be more aware. I recognise it is the 'slow-creep' of just one more thing that eventually tips the scales. The 'I know I shouldn't do it, but just this once' mentality and wham … it feels like you are right back where you started. A painful yet important reminder. The blessing is that I am not back where I started. Instead, I am fully armed with the vibrant colourful wisdom that I have gathered along the way. My mind and body know how to heal!

Sometimes each of us needs a little universal nudge to notice the signs that our body is sending us. Now … *Are YOU listening?*

My message is clear. We must never become complacent. No matter how far we have come, no matter what we have learned. While we walk this earth, we are all students; here to experience, here to learn.

Labels are far less important to me now; however, it took over thirty-five years to finally get a diagnosis that fitted what had been happening to me. After many misdiagnoses along the way, I was finally diagnosed with an autoimmune disease called psoriatic arthritis. Autoimmune disorders are currently on the rise in society at a disproportionate rate to population growth. A major trigger is stress. Poor diet, lack of exercise, lack of restful sleep, even smoking, are other implicated factors. These things we can do something about. It is essential to take our bodies out of fight-flight/stress mode to allow for natural healing to occur.

When we decide to remain vigilantly aware of the signs and messages our body sends us, it is simply a matter of resetting our intention to be what we 'choose' to be, and focusing our powerful attention on the solution, not the problem. Your focus of attention is like a powerful torch light that illuminates and strengthens whatever you shine it on. If you shine it on pain, you will find more pain. If you shine it on limitations, you will find limitations. Now imagine the intelligence so powerful that it knows how to create a human body, that does trillions of intricate functions every minute of your life. Now can you imagine what is possible when you direct that massive potential by shining your powerful attention on your intention to heal or create something of value; sending a potent message to the powerful subconscious mind that already knows what to do?

I no longer pin my hopes on others to heal my body. Preferring instead to dive deep into the pool of my own resources, knowing, trusting, and believing in the power and potential of the human mind and body to heal, as I take full responsibility for my emotional and physical health.

I love my body for all the lessons it has provided me, and I love life; I now stand in the rain, chase rainbows, notice butterflies and dream big with no limitations.

This doesn't mean I always get it right, far from it, but daily self-care is my practice and priority. I still occasionally get a tap on the shoulder ... *Are you listening?*

YES. I am listening now.

Danielle Aitken is a highly experienced nurse, midwife, and now psychotherapist who is passionate about mind-body therapy, principles of neuroplasticity, epigenetics, and quantum physics. A staunch believer of the power and potential of the human mind and the written word, she seeks to educate and validate through her writing. Danielle is author of *Sarah's Story, Life After IVF,* and T*he Ripples, What Lies Beyond;* both fictional, inspirational narratives written to tackle serious issues impacting mental and physical health, whilst also exploring human potential to overcoming adversity. Both of Danielle's books have been gifted to A-list Hollywood celebrities and both have become No.1 Amazon Bestsellers in multiple categories.

Building Dreams, Finding Strength

by Sue Croft

I am sitting in my chair under my newly renovated pergola, reflecting on everything I have achieved since the day I left home as a naive eighteen-year-old. My story is one of achievement through determination in the face of challenges that were, and are still, relevant for many women today.

The year was 1975. I was marrying John on what started out as a beautiful sunny day. We were marrying in my parents' gorgeous garden in Sandringham. John's parents had tried to stop our marriage, making our special day feel like a storm cloud was hanging over us, but we were young and in love, and nothing was going to stop us from chasing our dreams.

We bought our first home in Hallam, Victoria. We had no idea where Hallam was, we were just out for a Sunday drive and looking at housing estates. The house we looked at was small and situated on the side of a gentle, rolling hill overlooking another hill with green pastures, gum trees and cows. The scene was beautiful, and the brick veneer house, though small, was lovely. Once we had signed on the dotted line, we asked the agent where we were. He said, 'This is Hallam, not far out of Dandenong.'

We moved in shortly before my twenty-first birthday. It was so exciting to have our own home and I was thrilled to be able to decorate it. I began work at once, cultivating a garden filled with sweet smelling flowers, shrubs and trees. Friends and family joined us to celebrate my birthday and brought along gifts for the house and garden.

Our son, Trevor, was born five years later in May 1980, twelve and a half weeks premature. He spent the first four months of his life in the Royal Women's Hospital and was not expected to survive, but he did, thanks to all the hard work of the nurses and doctors. He was such an active little boy who brought us many funny moments, and fears when climbing trees and fences. I came into his room one morning to find him sitting on top of the wardrobe. He had climbed out of his cot onto the dresser, then up the side of the small children's wardrobe. So, early on I knew I had to watch this little fellow as he was adventurous and a bit of a risk-taker. He learnt to swim early on, and his teacher would always comment about him being a little fish in the water because he loved it so much and would jump in every chance he could. When he was older, we would travel to field archery competitions and he got his first bow at ten, competing in the junior grades and progressing as he grew older. Today, Trevor is married to Sarah, they are looking to starting a family one day.

While Trevor was still small, my marriage to John was starting to fall apart. I was desperate to find a way to rebuild our relationship and, in my naivety, I thought that if we moved away to another area, we would have a fresh start and save our marriage. I started to look around for land and found a block in Rye on the Mornington Peninsula. It was a one-acre block of tea-tree-covered bushland. The road was unmade, there was no water, no power and no sewerage. We purchased the block and I started to design a house. I had seen large white limestone blocks being used in the houses around the Portsea area and thought they were so beautiful; I sourced them from Mount

Gambier, in South Australia. I designed the house as a large square with an internal courtyard which would be filled with plants and a fishpond in the middle, with seating in the corner. The rooms were arranged around the courtyard. Once my design was approved by the council we started work as owner-builders. In 1982 there was no insurance for owner-builders so getting the house built quickly was imperative in order to avoid theft of building materials.

Once we had sold the Hallam house, we purchased a former army tent to live in on the block while we built the house; it was so large that it could also store our furniture. We put up a makeshift shower – thank goodness it was a hot summer! We cooked all our meals on a gas BBQ. It was really roughing it but so exciting and challenging, we had never done anything like this before.

Once the concrete slab was laid, we began work on the limestone and John started to build up the walls. It was summer when we started our project; I would start in the morning wearing a tracksuit and by 9 am was stripping down to shorts and t-shirt, by 10 am I was in my bathers. Occupational Health and Safety was not heard of back then.

The limestone blocks were eight inches thick for the outside walls and six inches thick for the internal walls. John started laying the blocks around the concrete slab. As he was concreting the block together, he would place the steel strapping and work it up the block to the top where the roof would join the walls. The exterior walls needed to be edged to give a smooth surface around each block and the rest of the surface was chopped up with a tomahawk to give it a rough texture. I would edge the limestone block with an angle grinder that was powered by a petrol generator, once edged I would bolster the excess limestone off, leaving a smooth edge around the block. Using a tomahawk and hammer I would chop into the face of the limestone to give it the desired rough surface texture.

Limestone is malleable for about twelve months before it hardens.

We needed to do the 'line chasing', which are vertical and horizontal cut-outs for the plumbing pipes and for the electricity wiring early on, so we were ready when services became available. The interior walls were to stay smooth but required a light sanding and dusting off before painting. Firstly though, I had to do the placement line drawings by walking through the house and marking where power points, toilets and taps were to be placed. The angle grinder was used to cut out the lines where pipes and wiring would eventually go. After that I did the sanding and painting of the walls. Eventually, when the services were put in, the lines would be cemented over, sanded down and painted again.

I enjoyed every minute of this project and was excited to see my vision becoming a reality. It would be worth all the hardship and roughing it in a tent and the sweat, cuts and bruises that go along with building.

Once the Colorbond roof sheeting had arrived and the pine lining for the ceiling was ready to be installed, it was my job to carry the pine inside for John to put up. As I lifted the first plank, hundreds upon hundreds of huntsman spiders ran in all directions, finally finding refuge under the next sheet. I remember running on the spot, screaming. I was remembering my childhood, when I was playing Robinson Crusoe at my grandparents' home in Briar Hill, a semi-rural area in Victoria where I spent many school holidays. I lifted a steel sheet to build a shelter and huntsman spiders ran everywhere.

Once I had calmed down, and realising that the boards had to go inside before we got any rain, I proceeded to 'whip' the long boards first so all the huntsman spiders would go under the next board. Whipping the boards meant that I had to hold one end of the sheet which was three metres long and lift it up and 'whip' it so that the board would lift up all along its length then come down again. If I had just lifted the sheets in the middle the huntsman spiders would end up running all over me – too scary to think about, so I needed a way to get them off the board without them touching me – hence the 'whipping' action. Even though

I was scared, it was fascinating watching them move under the next plank. It was like a waterfall in motion. When I got to the last board, I walked away leaving all the huntsman's hiding under it, because I knew that if I lifted the last sheet they would have nowhere left to hide, and I did not want to be in their path.

After the roof was installed and secured, we moved everything from the tent into the house, even though we did not have a Certificate of Occupancy from the council. Once we settled inside the house, I began looking at what we needed to do to finish it. I purchased a huge AGA range that would provide our hot water, cooking and heating requirements. We also had a septic tank system installed.

In the summer of 1984, a massive storm hit the Mornington Peninsula and destroyed many houses; trees fell and boats were beached. Mornington Yacht Club members lost many of their yachts in the storm. We lost our roof, it was like Dorothy in *The Wizard of Oz,* I watched as the wind lifted the roof off and threw it in one piece onto the backyard. The sound was deafening. The force of the wind was so great that it dragged all the strapping that held the roof down from the base of the walls out of the wall cavity. The SES came and placed a tarp over the roof for me. I had no idea where John was and there were no mobile phones to be able to call him.

My girlfriend and her husband were coming down from Melbourne that day to visit. My girlfriend minded Trevor inside while her husband and I got on the roof and placed the unused limestone blocks over the tarp to hold it down, even though the SES had secured it as best they could. We were drenched and the wind was howling, the rain was lashing us, but we had to keep the tarp down to stop it flying off. In addition to the weather conditions, I have a fear of heights and going up and down a ladder on the outside to access the roof was terrifying.

After they left to go home, I waited for John to get back – I was getting cold and could not get warm – but as the day wore on and he had not arrived, I packed a couple of things, left a note to say I was going to my parents to have a hot shower and to give Trevor a bath. As I drove along the highway beside the beach the wind was pushing the sand and water up to the edge of the road, and sand was blowing all around. The campsites in Rosebud were torn apart and many of the caravans had been damaged.

After the clean-up, we started to finish the house. It was at this time that I realised our marriage was over, and I decided to leave. The decision to leave was not easy but I needed to take care of my wellbeing. Taking Trevor with me, and not much else, I packed my car and drove away, leaving behind my unfinished dream home – I was making a new start, but not the one I had planned.

I rented a two-bedroom unit for myself and Trevor and enrolled him in kindergarten. I knew I had to put a roof over his head, so when I found a new subdivision in Seaford North, I called and asked for the cheapest block, saying I would be there in a few days to pay the deposit. On Saturday I arrived at the site office and was told that the block of land was accidently sold by his manager the night before. However, the agent told me I could choose one of the remaining blocks for the same price. I went through the list and chose the most expensive one, it was located in a small court.

For the next two years I designed the house and floor plan. I would visually walk through the drawing and make changes to suit. It turned out to be a small version of the house I had designed in Rye. No courtyard, but that did not matter. What was important was the open floor plan. I was the onsite project manager for the job. Once the design was completed, my draftsman put in the size and measurements, and I chose bricks, plaster, kitchen fittings and bathroom fixtures. Once the plan was approved I coordinated the contractors; I was lucky enough to have tradesmen friends who did the slab, bricking and framework. I did all the painting and organising. The only trades that I used outside my tradesmen friends were the electrician, plumber, roof plumber and plasterers. In those days builders would hire the power pole and the portable toilet for twelve weeks, so I knew how long I had to get the house built.

I was lucky again. Just like the first home in Rye, it was a long hot summer and autumn, so work moved along quickly. Organisation of trades was the most important thing to arrange, so after all the quotes were received, I planned the start dates for each, then confirmed the dates and followed up three weeks out, then again one week out, then the night before they were due on site to start the job. As project manager I needed to be very well organised and to think on my feet, so that if there were any issues with the build I could communicate effectively with the tradesmen. All went according to schedule and I was able to achieve my project on time.

Sunday 5 June 1988 was the day before I moved in, and I needed to paint the walls and floor. The removalists were coming at 8 am the next morning. Unfortunately, at 6:30, as the plumber was finishing off the bathroom connections, the rain came and it did not stop. The removalist truck arrived and nearly got bogged in the mud, and the men carrying the furniture inside tramped mud all through the house – thank goodness it was only painted concrete floors throughout!

I also moved in without having my Certificate of Occupancy and was intending to complete the inside as I could afford it, which meant I had a makeshift kitchen and a bathroom without tiles for a while. Being a wet area, the bathroom was a priority, so I tackled the tiling job on my own. Never again! The bathroom had floor-to-ceiling tiles and there was a step up to the bath. The tiles were dark vintage green with small painted white flowers with a border tile at the top – it looked great when it was finished and only a professional tiler would notice any mistakes.

During the build, I had a roof plumber put up a Colorbond roof and downpipes. This is where I had a huge learning curve – roof plumbers do not connect the downpipes to the storm water pipes which meant that all the rainwater went over the land, no garden at this stage. Coming home from work late one night, I drove up the driveway and immediately my car sunk up to its axles in mud. It was time for a driveway, and for a garden to be designed and planted.

Ten years ago, I designed and owner-built an extension to my home; I wanted a craft room for my craft work and sewing. Later I would change the craft room into a sunroom because in the afternoon the sun warmed the room in winter and I could sit out there and read with a cup of tea. Part of this room has been divided so that I now have a small guest room for when friends and family stay over.

I have been in my home for thirty-two years. Four years ago I realised it required some updating, along with some serious maintenance. Where do you start? Usually with the area that requires the most work. For me, the bathroom – with all its beautiful tiles – had to be remodelled. When we are young, stepping up to a sunken bath that has a shower overhead is lovely but as we age it becomes dangerous. There was no way I was going to do any tiling – been there and done that! Once the design was worked through, I had the plumber remove all the old piping and put in new piping which also meant cutting into the concrete slab. I extended the bathroom into my laundry and had access from the bathroom to the laundry. The original laundry was quite large because I thought I would do my ironing in there. In thirty years I have never done any ironing in the laundry. The laundry is now a smaller room off the bathroom.

Again, I had floor to ceiling tiles, this time large white tiles and on the floor dark grey tiles the same size. While sourcing materials for the bathroom I came across a business that made custom timber furniture and cabinetry. I designed a beautiful bathroom cabinet in messmate timber to hold the two round ceramic basins.

Once the bathroom and laundry were finished it was time to look at the kitchen. I kept the footprint of the kitchen the same, replacing all the cabinets, changing cupboards to drawers and taking out the corner pantry which over the years proved to be a waste of space and a collector of 'stuff'. I like white kitchens with colour accents; now I have a beautiful kitchen with straight lines and a pop of colour. My Belling range is orange, and the splashback is a mix of hexagonal tiles in black, dark grey, light grey, and off-white which are tiled to the ceiling.

The 'danger' of renovating, or a better phrase might be 'when you get bitten by the renovating bug', is that it never stops at just one thing. After finishing the bathroom/laundry/kitchen, I looked out at my old flat-roofed pergola and thought that it was time to redesign and rebuild. And there began my next renovating project. Once designed, my tradesmen friends came and built it on the same footprint as the old frame. The roofline was changed from a flat roof to two gable roofs and an angled flat section. Once all the timber was delivered, I needed to paint it prior to the pergola being erected. I had two weeks to finish the painting; fortunately, the weather at the time was hot and dry. Towards the end I was painting from ten in the morning until six at night. I chose a dark blue colour for the paint and ordered two black outdoor fans with lights to go under the two gables. It is a beautiful area to sit outside and enjoy the garden, either on my own or with family and friends.

With the COVID-19 pandemic, Victoria was hit hard, with many cases of infection, and sadly, many deaths. Our Premier, Daniel Andrews, shut down the state and we went into months of isolation. I was grateful that all my renovating projects had been finished.

Being isolated has given me time to think about my next renovating project, a built-in floor-to-ceiling, wall-to-wall bookshelf. Once the renovating bug hits, it never leaves, and I am sure I will have more projects once the bookshelf is completed and stacked with all my books.

I wanted to tell this story of my two homes because I believe that you can do anything if you put your mind to it. When I designed my first home, I had no experience in the design or building field, but I had determination and a desire to prove to myself that I could do it. When I left my husband, I knew that I had to design and build another home as an owner-builder. It was important to me that my son had his own home to grow up in. The second home I designed is a cut down version of my first home because the block size was small compared to the first home's acre block.

One of the most important pieces of advice I can give anyone who wants to tackle an owner-builder project or renovating project is to be well organised, and to keep paperwork up to date, but most importantly it is to enjoy the adventure. I have made plenty of mistakes, but I have learned from each of them and can pass on that knowledge to other new owner-builders or renovators. I enjoy renovating and hope I never run out of projects. I have been in my home for thirty-two years and I would not change a thing. I am proud of what I was able to design and build from my first limestone home in Rye to my current home in Seaford North. I am grateful for the help of my tradesmen friends who helped me achieve my goal.

Building two houses, and extending and renovating the second, has helped to shape me into who I am today. My first home was built by a young naive woman who was trying to keep her marriage together. Although the marriage didn't last, my confidence grew and I felt empowered by my success. As a single mother, I built my second owner-builder home, determined to face life on its terms. I am proud of my accomplishments, which I am happy to say, are many, but as an owner-builder I not only provided a comfortable and safe home for my son and I, but also lay strong foundations for my future endeavours.

Sue Croft is a writer and researcher. She has a Bachelor of Arts with a specialization in History. Born in Sydney, New South Wales, she is now living in Seaford North, Victoria. Sue took up field archery in her twenties and competed for twelve years, coming third in her grade in the National Titles held in Ipswich, Queensland.

The Colours of Me is Sue's first contribution to an anthology. She is currently working on a manuscript about a First World War soldier and his family back home in Australia, which will focus on the social history from 1912 to 1919.

A bird sitting in a tree is never afraid of the branch breaking, because her trust is not in that branch but in her wings.

— Author unknown

Thriving – Moving Beyond Trauma

by Jacquie Walker

I really want to share with you the wonder and joy of my life's journey. My understanding and way of viewing life are continually growing and expanding, and I feel like I am standing on the top of the mountain after completing a long trek.

As I look around me, all the views come together and I see how they all fit together and support each other, providing me with a new context for understanding my trauma story and increasing my sense of self. Major trauma events in my life include rape, sexual abuse, emotional abuse and mental abuse. I was diagnosed with PTSD by my doctor after seeking counselling and looking for a support group in my community. I experienced regular night terrors and body memories that would show up during waking and sleeping hours. I was too afraid to sleep for long periods, so I managed on catnaps for many years. One of the side effects is hypervigilance, and to some degree this is still an ongoing issue.

As part of my healing journey, I found online groups where I was able to share my story and listen to the stories of others who had similar trauma experiences to me. This was the place where I found the courage to look at what haunted me.

At the heart of it all is my spiritual journey which has been continually growing and reshaping the way I see and connect to the world – my understanding of spirit, and my capacity to trust and give unconditionally.

As I explored and continued my journey, being connected with a community helped me grow more and more into who I am. Part of my self-realisation has come from participating in healing and transformational workshops; from my connection with professional organisations; from presenting to colleagues; and from the support and feedback given by friends along the way.

Why would an intelligent and attractive woman find herself trapped in a cycle of abuse? Life happens to us and we are the product of our life experiences in our family, our home, at school and in the community that we grew up in. These all influence and shape our world view through our shared experiences and the messages both explicit and unspoken.

Growing Up

I was born in a small country town in south-west Western Australia and grew up on a farm twenty miles out of town. My dad delivered me into this world at the local town hospital, as the town doctor had gone away on a fishing trip. Our farmhouse had a kitchen, lounge room and two bedrooms. We had a radio, a kerosene fridge, a diesel generator that provided electricity for the house, and a water tank.

My memory of my mum is very scant as she did not really engage with me as a child. Maybe it was the nature of the birth and the stress or living so far out of town, but right from the beginning my mother was absent, long before she left the family home. She was probably suffering from postnatal depression. My dad recently shared with me that mum never fed me as a baby during the night. He was the one who got up and gave me night feeds and saw to it I was changed into dry nappies. We have family photos that show me being weighed in the shearing shed as mum refused to go to the mothers' clinic. I do remember her getting hysterical at times when she felt under pressure or was uncertain. When this happened, my dad would always come to the rescue. She spent most of her hours completing the house chores and then the rest of her day was spent escaping into the world of her novels while she smoked and drank sherry. During those times we were told to play outside.

As a young child I spent many hours walking paddocks, following sheep trails, and playing with imaginary friends. I had the company of my brother who was a year younger.

Before the age of five I had little contact with the wider world. What I did have was a deep connection to the land. My first experience of being in a community larger than my extended family was when I started attending kindergarten and primary school. This was a difficult time for me as I was not used to following rules or mixing with so many people. I was shy and kept to myself. I was picked on by older boys as they objected to the ribbons that my mother tied in my hair. A small taunt – but the impact was the first of many that collected during my childhood at the hands of fellow students, who found me an easy target to bully.

Shift

When I was seven, we moved to Perth. Mum and Dad bought a newsagency in a 'nice' suburb that was in a social housing area. This turned out to be a decision that had a big influence on my future wellbeing and mental health. The move was a culture shock and I never quite belonged in that school environment. I withdrew and kept to myself. I did not make friends easily.

Mum and Dad had terrible arguments that, unbeknown to both, us kids heard and internalised. When I was ten our family broke apart. The change came when Mum returned from an overseas holiday. Two weeks later Mum left to live out her *Shirley Valentine* fantasy in Greece. I guess she realised that we would be okay without her.

This brought radical change in all our lives. We were ostracised, as her leaving was scandalous. School became a nightmare, a place where I was bullied. At home there was little emotional support as we were all dealing with our own crisis. My dad provided for us on the physical level and was not capable of more. The advice given was to toughen up and not let others see they were upsetting you. I learnt to hide and deny my feelings.

The transition to high school was difficult. I ran into peer group pressure. My way of escaping was to put all my effort into my school studies, dancing, gymnastics, and reading. My dad always had high expectations of me, so at the same time I was hiding what was happening at school, I was striving to get good results to please him. If I got good grades, I had his praise. This was like an elixir.

When I was fourteen I found a babysitting job to earn some money for clothes, shoes, and cigarettes. The lady I babysat for became a shining light and mentor in my life; she gave me the gift of hope. She was one of first people who really acknowledged my presence, showing an interest in me. Through kindness and compassion, she reached out to me. She encouraged me to step out of my comfort zone, to try new things and to stand up for myself. This was hard for me. She taught me that I had choices and that it was possible to build a positive life.

Life then took another spiralling turn. When I was sixteen, I was sexually violated. This life-altering event left me feeling unclean and shamed and I never mentioned what happened to anyone.

Depression was a daily battle. Giving in to peer group pressure, I found that by compromising my beliefs and values I could find acceptance. By some miracle and much determination, I managed to finish my final year at school. I just scraped a pass and had enough points to be accepted into teachers college. Becoming a teacher was a long-standing aspiration of mine, to teach other children like me, to be the teacher that I wished I had, who would step in and make things right.

As time passed, my mother reconnected with the family. She organised to come to dinner once a week. This continued until I left home to go teaching. Once I had my licence, I would drive Mum home after the family dinner. That was when life took another turn into darkness and shame. I experienced sexual assault episodes with my mother's partner from the age of nineteen. Later, at the age of twenty-two I would meet my husband-to-be, and he too would become an abuser. During this time in my life, I lived with depression and mental stress that greatly impinged on every aspect of my world, and I developed what I call my 'sliding door memory'. It was also the beginning of a lifetime of searching for self and answers.

When you are experiencing trauma, anger and rage is often projected onto others. Anger and rage are not to be feared. It is important to allow the individual to express all they need without interrupting or trying to divert or reshape the outpouring. This is the beginning of the release that leads to real healing.

My healing journey has been ongoing. Much of my childhood trauma found healing in the context of my role as teacher over a thirty-year career. In building relationships with many children, I saw images of my younger self. I was able to indulge my inner child in play and fun-filled experiences that also became learning experiences. Through responding with empathy, I was able to bring positive change and love to otherwise traumatising life events in the context of school bullying for many children.

The first major steps that opened me up and led me to the pathways towards healing were learning reiki and meditation. I learnt to work with my mind to stop the internal panic and fear – which gave my mind a break. At the same time I was learning karate; the sparring practice sessions, hitting and kicking the punching bags helped to channel my rage and frustration at life and to release the pent-up emotions. It was very liberating. The great synergy was in finding a way to work holistically, with the mental, spiritual and physical body. My higher self was working to help me move beyond my past.

The other gift that has followed me all my life is my connection to nature and the land. In natural landscapes, I find deep connection and communion. I particularly feel at home in wilderness, far from the cities and towns where I can be immersed in the timeless energy of the place and connect to the marvel of the life and inherent beauty. The oceans, forests, and desert landscapes have become my personal safe place, and over the years have provided me with sanctuary and healing.

Feeling safe in a space away from the chaos I was living in was the key to all future healing. As I began to connect to myself in loving ways, I realised the abusive nature of the marriage I was living in and began to see the restraints and ties which were intended to hold me in fear.

The inner battle raged until I collapsed, and my life fell apart. Everything changed. I left my marriage.

Reclaiming myself and life

I attended CoDA (Co-Dependant Anonymous) 12 Step meetings every Tuesday for two years – never missing. I had the record for best attendance. The gift of the CoDA meetings was in the routine. Each person had time to share without being interrupted and free of judgment. The 12 Step program assisted me to look at how I related to others and the world, providing me with the space and opportunity to look at life through a new lens and to take responsibility for my life.

I fell into a relationship during this time with a man who loved and adored me. He was much older than I. At the time I felt I was in love with him, but this was in fact the shadow of myself. He encouraged me to take the journey and follow my instincts and gave me support when I felt discouraged. He helped me to find confidence in myself and introduced me to a new world, where life was bright and free from fear. I found acceptance and I was encouraged to explore who I was becoming.

I spent another seven years working weekly with a psychologist followed by a further three years monthly to keep me on track. During the weekly sessions we would look at the issues arising in my present time and at how my reactions were being influenced by the trauma of my past. The key to healing was finding the patterns that held me in the spiral of illusion, frustration and anger at life, that held me in the never-ending cycle of repetition. We would then look at the feelings that were surfacing, allowing the memories to surface and be witnessed. This was a process of connecting the dots and remembering and working through fear, shame and guilt.

I participated in dance and art therapy. This was most helpful for releasing body memories. The facilitator would pose questions and ask us to draw, paint or write a response while listening to music. Then we would dance the feeling to music, capturing the mood while connecting to the emotions that were presenting. Another powerful experience was psychodrama, portraying scenes from the past with significant others in role-play.

Following my spiritual pathways, I found 'sweat lodge' ceremonies (similar to rebirthing rituals) helped me move to another level. Beginning with an intent which you take into the process of facing fears. The heat intensifies during the ceremony and the challenge is to manage your emotions and breath, taming the heat and working with it rather than fighting it. You leave the lodge reborn, leaving layers of the old self behind, like when the snake sheds the skin it has outgrown. For a time, this healing journey felt like jumping into a pit with vipers – but gradually healing happened for me and I felt myself in a new way. As I became stronger and stepped into my own light embracing my talents and gift, I emerged a changed person. The textbooks call it a paradigm shift.

Many people are afraid of talking about abuse and of becoming involved with someone like me when I was experiencing the full effects of PTSD. When I was angry with the whole world, I pushed almost everyone away. Through Tao, I have come to understand that anger and rage are part the healing cycle. The imagery that helped me shape my view of life is of being in the flow of the river, in which the water finds the path of least resistance when it meets a boulder blocking its way.

Freedom at Fifty

At fifty, my realisation was that of self-love, acceptance and stepping into the power of Jacquie, dropping the many masks I had constructed to protect and block out others who might be a perceived threat to my wellbeing. Once I walked through the wall of my fear, I let the internal fire burn away the decades of built-up pain and anger. Letting go of the head talk and dropping into my heart, allowed me to connect with myself in the loving and empathic way, with the same love and empathy I gave to others. I found peace with my past. I found personal freedom to be truly myself. Since this time, I have found my life partner, a beautiful woman who I love and adore. Before I found this healing, I would not have been open to this loving relationship and would surely have pushed it away. Today, I do not hide from anyone. When invited, I share my story with others. I hope that my story will empower others to find acceptance and peace with their own life traumas that hold them in stalemate patterns.

The final step in my healing journey was to be open and transparent with my dad. I finally came to a place where I was not afraid of being judged or feeling the need to justify myself and my beliefs. And what I found, was that there was never really anything to be afraid of. The rules from my childhood never existed in my adult world. It was a fear-based story I had built upon the memory of my inner child in response to the chaos of the trauma in the family. The best gift that comes out of this life journey is a deep knowing of self and the inner awakening to my soul journey in this lifetime and finding the freedom to be my authentic self.

Jacquie Walker is an educator with more than thirty years of school-based experience; she is also the co-editor of a leading Australian magazine. Jacquie facilitates women's wisdom circles; meditation and workshops. Words that describe Jacquie include: passionate enabler, listener, witness and mentor.

Jacquie believes that real healing can and does happen through sharing our stories and by walking beyond our fear. Having walked her own journey, she is able to walk with others in theirs. She inspires and motivates those she mentors, facilitating real change gently with care and empathy.

Heal.
Your wounds will heal because that's what wounds are meant to do.
Your cuts and scrapes may leave behind scars, reminding you of that fall or break, but they will heal you and you will be stronger than you were before.
It is the same for heartbreaks and disappointments and failures.
They might sting now, they might make you sick to your stomach, they might bring you to your knees right now, but soon you will heal and be stronger than you ever were before.

— Walk the Earth

Tribute to an Angel
by Michelle Weitering

My lungs were on fire as I fled the scene of the crime, trying to comprehend what had just happened. I wondered if, when I reached my mother, I would live to see another day. Never in my life had I hurt anyone, let alone put an axe through someone's leg! My God, karma was going to bite me on the arse big time! How did it all go so wrong, so fast?

The image of my twin laying limp and pale at the bottom of the gumtree with the axe in her leg, blood leaking out of the wound flashed before me, making me gag. I fought against the black and white spots that began a gleeful jig behind my eyelids as they screamed at me … 'You're going to pass out.' I sucked in a lungful of air to chase the dizziness away while I pumped my ten-year-old, shaky legs as fast as I could across the paddock, through the orchard, and towards the sprawling farmhouse.

The day had started off so well, it was just another ordinary, uneventful

Saturday. The skies were grey when our stepfather woke us before heading off to work. As usual, he needed to open the tiny post office in Woolsthorpe, in the Western District of Victoria for the local farmers.

We got up to tend to our chores before breakfast, and to feed the orphaned calves and baby lambs their bottled milk. We were still half asleep ourselves, but the early morning start was made bearable by their sweet slurps. The lambs wriggling their curly tails eagerly as they guzzled the warm liquid, and the calves dribbled long lines of saliva as their large tongues probed the rubber teats, their gorgeous doe-like eyes staring into ours with gratitude.

After the bottles were drained and pats were given, we headed across to the chicken coop to crack the ice sheets that covered the water dishes during the chilly night. We collected the eggs and rescued the baby chicks that were half-frozen and close to death. We carried them inside and Mum placed them on a baking tray lined with a thick towel, then slid them into the bottom of the woodfire oven to defrost, leaving the door open. Eventually their little chirps would let Mum know they'd baked long enough and were ready to go back to their mother hen.

I remember the first time I watched Mum stuff a batch of frozen-feathered chicks in the oven, my eyes nearly balked out of their sockets, thinking, 'What *is* she doing?' Mum patiently explained the mechanics of safely defrosting a half-dead chicken.

Once the dog and cat were fed, it was our turn to choke down our bowls of porridge made with love, but foul in its stodginess all the same, before the rest of the morning jobs continued and then, it was time to be a kid. All in all, a typical start to a non-school day.

Looking back at the incident with the axe, I wonder why, if I were the one wielding the weapon, did I run like a bat out of hell to get away from my twin and escape whatever it was she had planned for me? The memory reveals to me that, even at ten years of age, my twin was a force to be reckoned with. So like our mother.

I remember scrambling up the tree, clinging to the axe as I stared down at my twin, who was bellowing at the top of her lungs, but it was all just white noise to me, as her mouth flapped open and closed. I was terrified that she was going to climb up after me, take the axe off me, and who knew what? That's when it all went so horribly wrong; my nervous, sweaty hand released the axe as I clung to the branch that swayed in the wind. I watched as the axe fell in slow motion towards my twin below and watched as she stumbled backwards in an attempt to get out of its way. I froze like a deer in the headlights as she tripped over a tree root and fell flat on her back the axe slamming into her shin bone.

She looked up at me, blessedly silent, and I think in that moment our twin expressions reflected each other's. Shock, and bewilderment! Her startled rabbit eyes, caught in the trap chased out by the ferret, dropped to the axe sticking up out of her shin bone, before passing out cold.

I practically flew out of the tree, paused over her pale limp body for a second as the metallic smell of blood filled my nostrils, then made the frantic journey back to the farmhouse. Mum was in the kitchen baking when I tore through the screen door. I remember her wearing brown corduroy pants and a green turtleneck sweater that was dusted in a light coating of flour. Within five seconds of me crying about what had happened, she marched past me and went outside towards the woodshed, took hold of the wheelbarrows handles with her flour coated hands and ran towards the paddock where the gumtree stood, with me in tow.

Mum began calling my twin's name as she reached her, slapping her gently on the face before scooping her up and plonking her into the wheelbarrow, turning it around and heading back in the direction we had come. 'Bloody hell, Mickey, what were you two up to?' Her voice held an anxious vibe as it shook in both anger and fright. I was unable to respond.

The axe had fallen to the ground, blood staining its tip; I hesitantly picked it up before trailing miserably behind Mum. Watching my twin's limp body flopping about in the wheelbarrow resembling a bowl of jelly had me filled with guilt. It took us a few minutes to get back to the farmhouse. I was surprised to see Mum veering towards the swimming pool, and even more surprised when she pulled the cover back to dump my twin unceremoniously into the not quite pond-green pool, left unmaintained in the winter months.

My twin regained consciousness, and then boy, did we both receive an earful. Poor Mum had been fighting against her own tears of fright, and once she knew my twin was okay, we got lectured till the cows came home, and considering we lived primarily on a sheep farm, that lecture continued for quite some time.

My mother was thirty years old when that incident took place, and for the decade before that, her life had been challenging to say the least. Born in 1952, the middle child of five, she worked hard for her place in a busy family. She attended an all-girls school called Preston Technical and worked weekends at Nelson Hardware for four years in Preston and Northcote. Being a nurturing soul, she ventured into nursing at Fairfield Hospital, and at the age of nineteen, met and married our father, who had the power in those days, to insist that she drop out of her nursing training just three weeks before graduation day. She then got a position at the Leader Publishing Company in Thornbury and worked her way up, from front counter girl to an editorial position, which made her incredibly proud.

Mum once shared with me that the day my twin and I were conceived was one of the darkest days of her life. The word 'raped' was used, despite the fact that they had just been married. It breaks my heart that she suffered so, and that her journey forward was one of heartbreak and abuse. She also shared that the day my twin and I were born was the best day of her life, despite the fact that we were two months premature, and she had to return home without us. She claims that was the second worst day of her life, the first being the day she married our father.

The day she brought me home to Baxter from the Royal Women's Hospital in Carlton, Melbourne, she received a broken nose from my father, along with a black eye and broken ribs. He had taken out his fury at being dishonourably discharged from the army on her whilst she was trying to bottle feed two tiny babies. She put up with his abuse for two more years, before bravely divorcing him. Divorce in the era of 1974 was filled with shame and embarrassment, yet she took that step towards the light to better her life.

Sadly, she ended up with a man double her age, and although he did not physically abuse her, she was subjected to decades of mental abuse and manipulation. Despite all those hardships, she was pure kindness wrapped up in smooth, fair skin, the brightest of blue eyes, the warmest smile, and a gorgeous mop of wavy red hair that revealed both a fiery temper and the most vibrant personality. She was, to me, absolute perfection.

Like any close, mother-daughter relationship, her battles, losses and wins in life rubbed off on me, and I saw the world in a different light because of all she had endured, and survived, without complaint. We were strong, resilient country women with hearts of gold that had plenty of room for forgiveness and patience, but no tolerance for dishonest bullshitters.

Whilst working full-time as the supervising cook for close to forty years at the May Noonan Hostel in Terang, Mum supported my twin and I in all our endeavours. When I finished high school and began working in child care, then falling in love with and marrying my soulmate, Mum was there to cheer me on every step of the way. A few years later it was an absolute joy to watch her became the most dotting Nana ever to our nephew, and then to our two beautiful boys, followed by her first granddaughter. Our friendship blossomed as the years passed and my own awareness and gratitude grew for all she had given to my twin and I growing up. She did the very best she could with what little we had; this became more apparent as my own journey through motherhood continued.

When my husband, Jade, and I watched our two little humans battling with anxiety and depression, Mum showed me yet another side to her strength of character. Although, being of the generation she was, she didn't really understand what anxiety was, or how her grandsons fell to the silent predator that is mental illness, that did not stop her from diving in and wrapping her loving arms around us all. She selflessly poured her healing energy into our bruised, broken little family during the time when we felt lost, hopeless and overwhelmed, fighting to understand and deal with the disorder that stole a big part of our boys' childhoods. Despite her sadness and distress at seeing her grandsons' individual struggles, Mum's unyielding love, support and compassion shone through as she tried to understand what was happening. After losing her own mother and a dear sister, whilst dealing with her own grief and the ups and downs of everyday life, she continued to work in her full-time position at the nursing home. On top of all that, she was an absolute beacon of strength as she continued to support her two daughters and their children,

Just like the axe incident, she was calm in the face of the unknown, and only let tears fall once answers were found and healing began. She was my eldest son's number one fan as he struggled with life as a teenager, and she was his greatest confider when he did not think he could endure another day on this planet. She saved us all in more ways than one, as mothers have the gift to do.

Even though her heart must have been breaking into pieces dealing with her own grief, she remained strong and supportive as she watched me struggle and fall into despair. Feeling that I had failed my children crippled me for a short time. It was the same strength she showed while raising me that pulled me out of my dark hole and back onto the light of life, enabling me to do what I had to do, to be all that I could to help my boys.

And that's motherhood, isn't it? It is an invisible cloak that we wear, that shields us from our own pain, past and present, enabling us to continue marching forward in life, to be that tower of strength for the small humans we brought into this world, no matter their age as the years fly by.

The day Mum passed away I felt such a shift in my energy, and not for the first time, I understood the phrase 'out-of-body experience'. Someone had turned off the lights, and I was alone in a dark cave, before claustrophobia became my companion, stealing all my oxygen, and Mr Panic Attack decided he wanted to sit with us too.

My soul had split in half in order to survive my crippling grief. I was so numb in my disbelief that she had gone, yet flooded with so many painful emotions, years filled with memories and conversations bombarded me. For forty-eight hours straight, I did not sleep.

How does one survive the loss of their mother? For forty-four years, she had been my first, my last, and everything in between: mother, best friend, supporter, confidante. Trying to describe all she was to me, the list truly is endless. The unconditional love of a mother is one of the most powerful things in this world, and despite the fact that my childhood had so many elements of trauma to it, I wouldn't change a thing, because I was so blessed in this life, to call her, Mum.

I began writing a journal to Mum, the day she passed. My sons, husband and nephew had all gone to bed, and I sat in the darkened lounge, lit by a lone candle. I sat right near the window where she had unexpectedly passed away that Boxing Day morning as I had explained to the paramedic that Mum had lost the ability to speak. I should have been holding her hand.

Feeling nothing, yet feeling everything, I sat in my disbelief that she was gone. Numb, lost and not knowing the dark, soul-shattering path grief was yet to walk me down. Silent tears drenched the first page, as treasured memories flowed. A lifetime of memories. Dancing to Abba with Mum and dear friends, hearing her laughter as she cherished every single occasion we celebrated over the years. Her voice, her advice, her encouragement. Her. Just her. Writing to her in that moment allowed me to feel that she was with me still.

> *Day one of 'the day.' The day you left me, Mum. And I miss you already. I miss you so much. It's 3 am. I cannot sleep. I do not want to dream in a world without you. I won't allow myself that one small comfort of slipping into oblivion, to surrender to the darkness that will give me ten minutes peace so I can forget. Forget that I will not hear your voice when I wake. Forget that you are no longer beside me on this earth. Forget that I will not be able to wrap my arms around you, my dearest friend, and tell you how much I love you. I long to hear you laugh and reply, 'I love me too!' To hear you say my name, the name you gifted me with. Oh, Mum! I would give anything in this world to talk to you right now, even if only to hear one of your lame jokes that you delighted in telling!*
>
> *The finality of death really doesn't hit us, until it does. And then, one last breath, it's over, followed by a sea of unbearable, crushing pain. Oh. That. Endless. Pain. Your death hasn't just hit me,*

Tribute to an Angel

Mum. It's knocked me over. Wiped me out. A tsunami of sorrow. Pure devastation that has reached its sharp, unsympathetic claws inside my chest, desperately searching for my shrunken soul, only to find my once big heart shattered into a million tiny, bruised pieces, crushing it further. I will grieve you forever. I know this. And the heaviness of that knowledge in this moment; irreparable. I miss you with every breath that I take, everything that I am ...

I wrote to her seeking comfort. Hoping it would bring me some sort of closure, only to find there was none, nor would there ever be. I was informed in those early days from friends who had experienced the death of a loved one, that grief was like a backpack, and every day, I would have to strap it to my back and carry it everywhere I went. Some days it would be filled with boulders, and every step forward would be crippling, and I'd feel as if I couldn't go on. Other days, it would feel as light as a feather: but always there for me to carry with me, every step for the rest of my days.

And that is the price we all pay to be human. To love and live this beautiful life that is a such a gift to all whom embrace it fully. As the foggy days rolled into weeks, then months and years, the skies brightened and each breath I took didn't hurt so much without her.

In a blink of an eye, four years have passed, Mum, my little red fox, and I miss you still. Desperately. Some days, I miss you more terribly than others, but always, miss you. The scent of Oil of Olay on a lady's paper-thin skin at the supermarket, brings you back to me. The waft of my nephew's cigarette smoke. An orange butterfly gracing my garden, that you adored sitting in. Your spaghetti bolognaise recipe, simmering on the stove in my tiny, outdated '70s style kitchen. The call of cicadas at Christmas time, as the Australian sun warms the earth. Every day. Always. A scent, a photograph, a voice, hell, my voice, an Abba track, and God help me, the Carpenters. True gifts, as they all bring you back to me. The best gift of all is when you visit me in my dreams, Mum. Then, I wake as tears of joy flow, before the image of you fades, like age steals memories. I go into the bathroom to wash away my tears, glancing reluctantly towards the mirror. I stop and force a smile, and then, there you are! I see you! In my grin, my cheeky smile. There you are! And there you shall always be, Mum, until I take my last breath.

The never-ending cycle that comes and goes in waves. Birth. Celebration. Adventure. Love. Pain. Joy. Loss. Heartache. Life and death and every single event in between. It all ebbs and flows, Mum, and time has made missing you easier; to float along, drifting peacefully in the current of life. My life, that you gifted me with. I will not waste it. I will make you proud.

Love always and forever. Mickey. XX

Yes, moving forward in a world without my mother physically by my side has been one of the most challenging things I've ever had to do, whilst carrying my grief and wearing a smile. Missing her as we celebrate birthdays and milestones, and not being able to hear her words of advice or encouragement in times of hardships isn't always easy, as we each live with the grief and hollow pain of losing the matriarch of our family.

Yet, I have always been a celebrator of life, and because of my great love and respect for her, and my gratitude for the life she gifted me with, I strive to focus on the joy of life around me, and along with my darling husband and sons, my twin and best friend, we celebrate her by cherishing each other, and by making every moment count.

I have searched and found the magic of Mum's presence everywhere and fill my cup with the joy and comfort of celebrating her in multiple ways, every single day.

Like Mum, my green thumb has created luscious gardens around our home. Vegetables and fruit, ferns and tropical plants, cottage and glasshouse gardens provide gifts for all who spend time with us, welcome to bask in a feeling of serenity and calm, before leaving with a basket full of fresh produce. Mum's generous nature fills my heart, and her love of animals echoes in my soul. The tick of her Grandfather clock is the heartbeat of my little Writer's Manor, where I fill pages that she would have loved to have read.

I can still remember the day she held my first book in her hands. The word 'proud' doesn't cover it. She was beyond elated, and now, when I write, I hear her voice and laughter in my mind as I plot away and make my characters live colourful lives. She would definitely say … 'Good one, Mickey!'

My biggest fan.

I feel blessed to see her everywhere. If not in a photo, in the faces of her grandchildren, in myself and in my twin.

I whisper hello to her whenever I glance up at the man in the moon in the night sky, and when the breeze carries the scent of rain towards me I smile and think of Mum, at home in Glenormiston, where she lived a full beautiful life surrounded by friends who loved her dearly. She truly was one of a kind, a most unique lady who has left the most remarkable footprints.

As I finish off my batch of tomato relish and fig jam, my heart is full as happy memories float along with the scents from the past, with a sense of fulfilment and gratitude for the life I have lived, and the years ahead that I have to look forward to, because of her. In my world, the glass is always half full, because of the passionate, hardworking, fun loving, well-read woman who raised me. I am so blessed she was my mother. What an honour to be her daughter. I truly am the colourful individual that I am today, because of her.

Michelle Weitering is a passionate mental health advocate who writes fiction and non-fiction titles as a voice for those living with mental health, domestic violence and other social issues. Michelle is currently advocating for Mother Earth under her pseudonym, Mickey Martin, in her soon to be released novel, *Soul Keepers of Glenormiston South,* a paranormal romance with ecological messages.

Facebook: michelleweitering
Email: mickeyslba@hotmail.com
Instagram: @mickeymartinbooks
Website: www.mickeymartinauthor.com

*Spring Sang Softly
As Winter Died
"I'll Bloom For You;
While My Heart Still Cries."*

— Angie Weiland-Crosby

The Balance of Colour in Conscious & Subconscious

by Melissa Billman

Who am I?
These thoughts beckon me to see
from the layers of the earth
to the fragments in the sea
from the depths of my soul
as the inner light reaches
light comes pouring as it teaches
out of my being for all to see
in its completion, I am now colours of me.

Let's turn to the inside of my head … my brain … my mind. I'm not worthy. I'm not loved. I'm not believing of all these positive things other people are saying and doing. I'm not pretty enough. I'm not skinny enough. I'm not enough. I'm fat. I'm ugly. I'm useless. I'm downtrodden. I'm a sinner. I'm not great enough. I'm not acknowledged. I'm worthless. I'm a loser. I'm an idiot.

I could go on and on for hours from the ugly space that I've now created inside of my head. Nothing grows from this space. Only darkness and a vain identity are felt from the crevasse of the space. Hell, I don't even know how to create the space.

These thoughts, of which I am now writing, are how I had felt and thought for a large portion of this beautiful life. You see ... I am young at this point where I take you back in the journey. I can hear the soft, subtle cries of loneliness, sadness, I am different, someone please help me.

I knew I was different; I knew I was strange, and I knew I wasn't loved. These were some of the many thoughts that plagued my mind as a wee child. I know I am here for a reason; however, I have no idea what that reason may or may not be. Nobody likes me, nobody loves me, I'm not loved, nor am I appreciated. All I ever wanted was to be loved. The one thing, of which I did not know, is that love is within us from our Creator during every moment of every day and that fact begins in the beginning.

In kindergarten ... I lay on my lime green flowered towel ... we were able to choose the towel of our liking to bring to the kindergarten class so that we could lay on the towel during our nap time. The towel, to me, represented my favourite colour green. I thought the towel was special. Not because it was soft, because it wasn't - it was rather rough in nature, but it looked pretty. I've always had a special eye for what I consider to be pretty. It had dimension, with the daisies and the white and lime green colours. Thinking back, I now respect my introspective creative nature. My nature to bring all things to life in my beautiful mind. For me, a suppressed mind encompasses a dead being. I submitted to allowing those around me to form me for who they wanted me to be, never worrying about myself or what I might want, or who I wanted to be.

A compassionate heart of a young creative blossoms in the environment of which it is raised. As I take myself back to the lime green and white flowered towel, I can remember laying my head upon it. I can remember the thoughts of the inadequacies laying upon the towel.

The Balance of Colour in Conscious & Subconscious

Nobody liked me. I had two silver front teeth. I wore the same clothes day after day, or at least rotated only a couple of outfits. We didn't come from much. I was the oldest of four children. I was the first to experience everything ... and boy oh boy, little did I know that is exactly what I would do. Experience everything. I would experience EVERYTHING. A special child or a 'sensitive child' was thought to be different, even by the parents of the special child. Sensitive children don't understand what they are 'receiving', especially in environments of strict belief systems. We aren't taught to experience or receive as children, or in my case ... we aren't left open to receive our own answers, because we do not own our own answers until the formative stands are taken for ourselves along the way.

I write what is occurring for me in the moment. These thoughts tend to flow, and I will not block a state of flow for a message I am receiving. When we are in the flow and alignment therein, we are in our most powerful state. Our most powerful state is one of vulnerability and a baring of our soul. During the process of peeling back the layers and baring our soul, our subconscious thought patterns are brought forward for exploration. This is where peeling back layers can tend to get a little bit tricky. As we peel back the layers of our subconscious as adults, or at whatever stage we are healing, we are invited to take a look at our essence of ourselves in our rawest of forms. It is where we can accept and choose to love our being and our soul or reject our reality. Pivotal points in the outline of our subconscious are brought forth or stowed away. During suppression, when our thoughts and feelings are stowed, we tend to bottleneck our growth. The bottleneck causes us to feel all the thoughts of unworthiness. As soon as we stop stepping into our power by burying our underlying issues, we cause massive roadblocks in our development as human beings.

The style or form we begin to communicate with shalt be one of being in our power. Once we are standing in our power and stepping into the next power, we are in our most powerful form of being. Raw and uncanny essence includes humour, grief, sadness, pain, expression, formality, and exuberance. The eloquence of my writing is me in human form. Nonetheless, the eloquence of my writing comes from a state of spirit, a state of receiving spirit. The transformational state of receiving is not something to be underestimated. It takes a tremendous amount of grit and discipline not to mention the formality of being in a state of growth to be in a state of receiving.

Our earliest childhood memory ... What is your earliest childhood memory? When do we recount the earliest situation where we felt like we were different? You heard a portion of mine in paragraphs above. It is a reality to me that as soon as I begin to recount the experience many other experiences begin to flow. Experiences of which I haven't thought about in a lifetime, or at least what appears to be a lifetime. In order to express *The Colours of Me* I am taking you on a journey (one of many) including one situation where I am remembering with patience, love, and forgiveness of that beautiful, little, innocent being, who was laying her head on her towel during naptime in kindergarten. Something so simple, yet so beautiful to look back upon with love and appreciation, but foremost, with gratitude. I am grateful for a countenance of all that of which I experienced along the way. The loving genesis of the first childhood memory I brought forth. How different it felt, nothing is as it was before, and shalt never be again. Before what? ... One might ask. Before the evolution of the being.

As I transition these thoughts in remembrance of who I was, a symphony in celebration begins to occur. I graduated kindergarten and began life in a private Catholic school. I was the child who had silver front teeth and glasses to correct the stigmatism in my right eye. An experience happened at the age of six months where I would lose almost complete focus in my left eye. It is something I am still learning as an adult to embrace. I embrace the experience by reliving it with love, forgiveness and appreciation in being. It may not be easily understood as I write. Still, I know it shalt be felt. It has become and is my favourite state of being. A state which is present. Present in this moment and present in any moment thereby which comes my way. It lends an ear to all relationships and is keystone in the essence of our being.

I am one of those who listens in order to receive. I am a listener. The listening capability of our heart is where it comes into play in our being. A mere forty years after laying on that green flower towel in kindergarten, yes forty years later, as I begin to speak for the first time in over four decades … I speak by what is occurring for me. It is not prescript or pre-planned. It is literally the most conscious form of being due to the event I am listening to via heart in order to connect to my soul and the soul of those I have relationships with - to include those relationships not yet discovered. My subconscious is opened up and is flowering. Triggers are erased and recognised as my subconscious openly flows. The subconscious mind and veil are thinner in each moment of expression. I raise the question to myself as I write: How is it possible that a transformation such as mine could possibly take forty years to complete. Immediately, the left side of my frontal cortex is activated in asking the 'how'. I own all the experiences, every single one of them. I am no longer afraid of what anyone may or may not think of me. It is the experiences within the experiences that are now occurring for me. All my beautiful experiences painted in colour exactly the way I experienced them. I now get to operate from a conscious state of being while accepting anything that needs or wants out from my subconscious.

Then abruptly, I am taken back. All these experiences. Every. Single. One. Of. Them. I haven't always seen things in colour. Not in the literal sense. Most things occurred in black or white, in light or in darkness.

And this is where I shalt begin the journey with you into the light and the dark. The colour of my personality. It hasn't always been colours that have lit my life light. Or maybe I should say my life plight. Either way, I believe you have received the picture. Let's talk about the 'whiteness' for a minute. Growing up and being in my head was more than often a miserable place. The inner darkness of the demons haunted me as I stated above, for a large portion of my life. I would allow myself to role-play the light.

For example, when I would wake in the middle of the night being haunted by the demons that surrounded me (I could feel the heaviness of the room), I would escape the darkness by way of embodying myself in light. I would vision myself lying in a field of white daisies. As I tell this story right here, I close my eyes to take you in the vision of light. As I am laying in the field of the white daisies, the air is crisp. The light shines upon my being and I am warmed. I draw lighter light in by feeling the space I am filling in my mind and the warmth of the space. The mountains and the earth surround me, and I am grounded. At times, I rise above my body as I am laying in the field and gaze back upon myself. As I gaze back upon myself, I am grounded and surrounded by Creations and the blessings of those creations therein. The mountains, the grasses and the vision are growing, and I am open to receive the feelings of the love, warmth, and light. My heart is renewed, and it is at peace. These thoughts would relax me enough and allow me to fall fast asleep after being woken by darkness. It has taken years in training of thoughts between the light and the darkness to see the light in all situations. Pivotal behaviours and learning. All learned and exercised by being alone. Yes, now I know that I was never alone but there were times where I had continuously been, for a very long time … left alone. And, until we are alone and trapped inside our head we don't know what it sometimes takes to remove ourselves from inside our head. To remove those deepest darkest demons from our experiences out of our head.

The Balance of Colour in Conscious & Subconscious

Let's talk about the demons for a minute. Exploring the darkness is frightening to most people whom of which have never experienced the darkness. Now, I know, I know ... we have all experienced darkness in one form or another. Dark passengers attach to us in the form of spirits being attached to our beings when we are in the darkness. Different addictions placated and justified will attract those dark spirits. Often the attachment is of the dark spirits. This is my belief. Yes, the attachment to the addiction of the agreement inside the addiction. Either way it is an attachment. Furthermore, this might be too dark for your comprehension. Or maybe the darkness is something that is not talked about enough. The empathy for the darkness is a unique trait, if I do say so myself. The empathetic nature of this soul of mine has empathy for all of what is and has been written here. There I go again, acknowledging the feelings I am having for those whom of which carry dark passengers. The exponential growth that comes with knowing what is yours and what is not yours is only comprehensible on a subhuman level. I don't believe I am subhuman. I am who I am. I am walking spirit, talking spirit, fire-breathing spirit and, most of all, I am truth-telling spirit.

Let's talk about truth. Growth occurred only in micro-faceted phases when I refused to acknowledge my own truth. It took me forever to understand my own truth. IF there is any one thing, I AM in this life ... I AM TRUTH. I will never again hide from who I am because of refusing to see the truth. You see ... it is not only about the truth of who we are being. It is about the perspective of the truth therein. How we choose to see the truth is by that of how we live. Our truths shed light upon our beliefs. We live with no governor. It is kind of like all shackles and chains have been lifted and we are free to walk around, gather, hang out and ponder in our truth. Our creative spirit lies in the truth of our heart. Imagine walking through life telling yourself those little white lies that get you from one place to the next whilst never bathing in your own truth. Our truth is different for each of us, for … it is ours and ours alone.

Navigating the waters of our being. The waters that bebop to and from uncertainty to certainty. The limitless expression that of which is felt through pain and suffering. Have you ever sat and looked at yourself in a mirror and had a conversation with yourself? How does it make you feel to stare back into your own eyes, your own mind, your own soul? Let's connect for a minute to our third person. She is lovely. She is the grace where beauty grows. She has felt levels of pain incomprehensible to an average person. Her rules are her governess, and she dictates in love, majesty, and honour. The integrous nature of her spirit is Divine and shan't forgo the absence of acknowledgement for one minute longer. The golden locks that surround her physical body flow freely as does the detail-oriented, pathway-finding, emotional-feeling, earthly surrounding of her soul. The presence of her being is felt by all upon her Goddess entrance. Sweet as honey … her emotions are intact, and her mind speaks brilliance. Her vision is enormous. The impact of her soul shalt be felt for generations upon generations of living and learning. She is pioneering as she reaches for the gravitational pulls and the magnetism therein. Her dreams are the fortitude of her life. The experiences within the fortitude grant direction as she moves in valour. She wears the colour of purple on her heart. Loyalty is her contribution as she is a selfless servant. She is the lioness whom of which humans shalt remember.

Navigating the dark waters of our being. Here comes those thoughts. Yes … they are merely thoughts. What shalt I do with these thoughts that are occurring to me. Through the years I have developed and deployed many different methods for dealing with absurd, hurtful, self-demeaning, and all other thoughts that could demean myself or anyone else. When I see the thought entering my mind I used to be overcome with thoughts. In large part, I lacked the focus aforementioned. Regardless, as soon as my limited belief subsided. (YOU know, the one limited belief I discussed earlier in this story? Where I believed that I couldn't focus? Yes … as soon as I pushed that limited belief outside my head, that is when I began connecting to my subconscious via streams of consciousness and intentional behaviour). For example: I am able to see the thought entering my brain. The negative thoughts are acknowledged in their raw form and then in my mind with my eyes closed I force those thoughts to the right and out the door as I let them fall away to the earth. Those thoughts no longer exist in the moment when I begin practicing this mind control technique on myself. Our mind is an actual place where we can go to help our physical, emotional, and spiritual self any time of day, seven days a week, 365 days a year. I recommend checking in often, grounding yourself, and loving yourself as well as pushing anything that doesn't serve you and your higher being … pushing it the hell out of the way.

A tremendous piece this has been to write. As I look back upon my last three thousand words, I am overcome with a sense of growth, gratitude, and love. To be able to transcribe a message which will impact and inspire millions of human beings is like being handed a special gift indeed. The growth I have experienced as a human being in a space and time such as this shall be the diamond that slices the shape of freedom for myself and others one sliver at a time. In wisdom, I have learned through painstaking lessons the value of our word. The impeccability of our words shall never be lost in time. From the scared little child and a short story shared I have learned a fascinating bit about the resilience of my being. To visit a child as ourselves, from our childhood, and to be able to look back upon the confusion of the big soul that inhabited the little body, and to do it with loving and open arms is the strength in growth for me and my message here. Fear is not real. Our thoughts are not real. We simply operate from a perspective of what is occurring in the moment and that will always be our most powerful message in that moment. In intention, we shift the state of our being. When we dive in and take a look at the darkest passengers attached to our soul, we either find a darkness that we cannot overcome, or we CHOOSE to see the light. The choice in healing is always an opportunity that is presented to us from the Universe. It is a choice. It is all a choice. Every thought, every whisper, every moment, and every breath shape our destiny by us deciding. Inside of the decision is where the infinite power and absolute creativity of our heart is housed. The gifts and talents inside each and every one of us is the source for transitional and traditional states between our conscious and subconscious, our being.

I am lovely. I am worthy. I am power. I am abundance. I am strength. I am perseverance. I am destiny. I am unconditional love. I am soul. I am shocked. I am spirit. I am guided. I am intuition. I am light. I am peace. I am serenity. I am grounded. I am bold. I am centred. I am heart. I am kind. I am truth. I am sweet. I am graceful. I am forgiveness. I am humility. I am virtue. I am loyalty. I am kindness. I am valour. I am loving. I am earth. I am infinity. I am writer. I am a poet. I am leader. I am beautiful. I am sun. I am one. I am whole. I am enough. I am acknowledged. I am validated. I am courage. I am encouraging. I am inspiring. I am flowing. I am forgiving. I am beauty. I am bravery. I am confidence. I AM LOVE and I AM LOVED.

In love and respect,
Melissa J. Billman (The Combat Poet)

Melissa Billman is a wildlife biologist by education and a real estate agent by trade. She is a servant of hearts whose mission is to leave others feeling their significance. At a very young age Melissa developed a special relationship with God. Her mission is way bigger than she. Her passions include writing, distinctions in language, and poetry, encompassing photography into storytelling while bringing value through communication of heart. She encompasses a witty sense of human and an unconditional love and respect for all animals and human beings, and is a philosopher in her own right.
Melissa's handle is @thecombat poet.2

And as she fell apart,
Her shattered pieces began
to bloom
-blossoming until she became
exactly who she was meant
to be..."

Becca Lee

Becoming Me
by Patricia Lovell

If I could reach back through time, I would whisper to my seventeen-year-old self to not let what she was about to experience, towards the end of that year, drain all her confidence. I would whisper to her to courageously face her fears, to accept responsibility, and to not carry the darkness of self-doubt, of not being good enough, of guilt and a sense of wrongness into the years ahead.

I would whisper to her to release the effects of a lie told to her at age thirteen. I would tell her that the lie that others didn't want to be in her presence was born in jealousy. I would tell her to not allow this made-up story to fill her with doubts and fears about stepping forward, of being seen, of being welcomed by others. I would tell her to quickly heal the effects when they reappear without reliving and believing the lie repeatedly.

I would also whisper, yes, I know it is painful carrying the disappointment of her parents and not being able to continue her nursing training, even though her long-held dreams to become a doctor weren't supported – another disappointment. I would whisper that I know how hard it was that her parents had the power to prevent her from making other choices and insisting on arranging the quick marriage that her pregnancy dictated in their eyes. I would encourage her to move from this turmoil, and to allow, as quickly as she could, the light and joy of the new life she was carrying to shine through the murkiness of her feelings and emotions.

Then I would tell her that doors will open, and she will become a remedial therapist, and an intuitive healer, even a teacher, that she would guide countless others through their healing journeys, illuminating for them the power of their choice to accept the gift of who they are, and can be.

Would I point out that moving from her childhood role as the family peacemaker into her role as wife and mother would be a continuation of denying her own feelings, and that co-dependency does not make for a healthy relationship? Should I tell her to listen and follow through on all the suggestions of some others to stop being so damn nice, to cease finding fault within herself, to know that a time of gratitude for all her life experiences will come?

I know what experiences lie ahead, that will all be a part her pain of becoming real. These experiences will reveal the smokescreen of illusions, the lack of self-worth and love covering the vibrancy of her radiant Truth, rather like a tablecloth obscuring the beauty of a timber table's grain.

Will I tell her when those pivotal moments of change will arrive, and how they will provide her with new perspectives about herself, her life, and how to live it?

Can I encourage her and let her know that, in order to embrace the lightness of her being, she will first need to embrace the darkness?

If only I could whisper, regardless of how she has lived her life, and continues to do so, her innate joy and belief in the power of a smile will prove to be her overriding life force.

No, I will not tell her. Her life is about to unfold, and will take her to those moments of change and transformation, at exactly the right time.

Becoming Me

I arrived from the star's seeding into Mother Earth in January 1951. In 1984, I was given an opportunity to not only chose life, but also to re-evaluate the choices I had lived by, and to decide whether they supported me in being able to live a full and joyous life in which I could express, without fear, who I was and who I was yet to become. Or else, I could continue with the thoughts, doubts, and false beliefs I held about myself, that robbed me of any joy or ability to love myself first before sharing it with others.

I joined my Catholic family of origin as the youngest of three children, joining a sister and brother. My parents were among the battlers of the postwar years that were signified by a lack of money, but also emotional support — feeling words were not often bandied about in our household. At an early age I assumed the role of the family peacemaker and viewed it as my responsibility to keep everyone happy. This role, and my normally agreeable and accepting nature, often worked against me. It became a habit to not say how I was feeling. If I was angry or frustrated, I was quickly told, 'That's not like you.' It became easier to bury the need to speak up; I would even bury my tears, and I resolved to never allow anyone to see how they had hurt me. I saved my brother from many punishments which would have ended with him in tears. I was always begging my mother or father to not hit him and just send him to his room. I couldn't handle hearing him, or anyone, crying.

As that young child I blamed myself for my father's drinking. I thought I may have done something wrong that upset him, or I hadn't been good enough. Many times, when I knew he was at a club or hotel I would maintain an unknown vigil looking from my bedroom window, watching and willing his car to crest the hill that I had in my view. After he had, only then could I relax and let the tension go. The darkness of fear would lift, even though the sparks of my mother's anger would soon fly. That was preferable to the alternative if I had failed to will him home.

Being married so young didn't enable me to develop life skills to overcome my sense of wrongness and overdeveloped responsibility towards others. It would be many years before I could relinquish the guilt about being pregnant before marriage. I certainly hadn't been a good Catholic girl. Yet, whilst carrying this guilt and feelings of shame, I never once regretted the birth of my eldest son and joyously welcomed the arrival of his two brothers in the following years. As young parents, we did our best.

I loved being a busy mother involved in my son's play and activities. I volunteered wherever there was a need, as well as working part-time as an integrative classroom aide supervising children with special needs. I amazed myself and the teachers by developing many programs that helped to build confidence and joy in the children who were entrusted into my care.

The joy and confidence I found outside the home wasn't always replicated within our home. As time passed my husband descended into becoming a functional alcoholic. Once again, I found myself stepping into the role of taking the blame and assuming the responsibility for his need to drink.

No-one would know, he was like many alcoholics, becoming a house devil and a street angel. Over time it became difficult to deny the hurt, the put downs, the judgements, and the ridicule. As I was beginning to awaken emotionally and spiritually, I often shared some deep thoughts that were meaningful to me with my husband. He would ridicule whatever I had shared, only to overhear him later on sharing it with others, then basking in the praise of how profound he was. It was also becoming noticeable to me how often he would belittle me in front of our friends. When I challenged him on this behaviour, he confirmed that he wanted our friends to be more his friends than mine.

Over time it seemed easier to avoid standing out or shining in any way.

Unknowingly, at that time I was being prepared for what 1984 would bring. I was drawn to learn many different forms of meditation, which put me in touch with my buried feelings and with the knowledge that there was no right or wrong. My tears, which felt as though they were locked in ice cubes, slowly began to melt. I was learning that I held the key to how I chose to express my feelings.

A Myers-Briggs Type Indicator® course deepened my understanding of my personality and strengths. The facilitator explained to me that one aspect of my profile, the need to search and know and be more, could be either a joy or a burden. I must have accepted it as a joy, and I honour that point in time as the beginning of searching out ways to always be a better version of myself.

An Enneagram course took me to greater depths of understanding, providing clues of what to aspire to and how to heal life's low points. One of the animals representing my character was the eagle, the bird that flies the highest gaining a clear overall view. The other animal was the ant. I didn't know until then that ants can move substances many times greater than their own size, but the trick is to roll it downhill, not uphill. I needed to honestly face that I was pushing uphill, and it was me who kept adding a spoke to the flow of my own wheel of life.

Armed with some measure of self-awareness I slipped quietly into 1984. I turned thirty-three, and with Easter drawing near I laughed about my age being the same as Jesus' age at the time of his crucifixion. After that Easter weekend it wasn't pain that drove me to seek help, it was the sense of going in and out of consciousness. I was about to discover that my being alive was defying medical science. To say that news was a shock was putting it mildly, yet at the same time, was hard to believe. I was born with what amounted to having a broken neck. Since birth, the top of my spine was never connected, my muscles and tendons held my spine in place with the cranium. Something as gentle as a sneeze could have cut my spinal cord.

You may wonder, had I previously had pain? Yes, but I learnt to adapt and not complain. Yes, I had balance problems from time to time, but learnt not to mention this, especially to my mother who would say, 'Yes, I will take you to the doctor but if they find nothing wrong with you, watch out!' At that time no-one thought to take X-rays, and I thought everyone needed to support their head with one hand when they were tired.

Fusion of my C1/C2 using donor bone from my hip along with wire was proposed. You may think I would jump in and have surgery straight away, but I had many thoughts running around in my head. If I had survived thus far, couldn't I trust that I could continue without surgery? This was a time where even though I was attaining a stronger sense of self, I focused on the massive disruption of three weeks in a hospital that was two hours' drive from home, plus another three months in a stabilising device, to my family's routine.

A lightning bolt thought arrived, and with it a full understanding that I was being given the opportunity to choose between life or certain death. I chose life and from that moment I felt a powerful presence that supported me through this time of reconnection which stays with me even now.

The exact date of surgery was 11 October, and while I do remember that, I also recall what happened when I returned to the ICU after my surgery.

I experienced myself being out of my body, and observed a nurse touching points all over my body while exclaiming, 'I can't find a pulse.' I remember watching her, then slipping away thinking that if this was dying it felt nice. I was enjoying the 'tunnel experience' that is often spoken of, until I was surrounded by what I can only describe as an intense Golden Goodness. I only received a taste of this energy before I was brought gently back to my body by a smile, and as one happy nurse exclaimed, 'I found one!'

My new-found meditation skills supported me during my hospital stay. For two and a half of those three weeks I spent in hospital I was stabilised by sandbags on one side and then the other every two hours. During that time of stillness, the mantra running through my mind was 'I can no longer look a gift horse in the mouth,' and I wondered where my gift of life was going to take me when I was fully recovered. My instincts were telling me that I could no longer make myself fit into how others thought I should live my life. What I didn't know was how to move on, past the 'peace at any cost' mantra. Who would I be? I felt my fear of death had lessened its grip but living life still held many unknown fears about the journey I was embarking upon.

Self-confidence was still in short supply as I stepped out on this new journey, and ironically it took two powerful comments from two different nuns to help me untie the knots of the Catholic fear and guilt that held me captive. One was a Sister of Mercy with whom I began studying the Mystics and Creation Centred Spiritually. She related a story about how many times others, full of suggestions for her, asked her an oft-repeated phrase, 'Have you thought of doing this ...?' When the question became one time too many she replied to her hapless inquisitor with another question: 'Are you going to do my dying for me?' Of course, that elicited a confused response, to which she replied to her own question, 'Then if you are not going to do my dying for me, then don't try to do my living for me.'

The other comment was made by Colleen, a Sister of St Joseph, who had become a very good friend. Prior to surgery she was the one who taught me meditation and so much more. If you have any preconceived ideas of what a nun is or isn't, none of them would apply to this amazing woman. Three years post-surgery she introduced me and a small group of others to 'A Course of Miracles' coining the phrase, 'God doesn't give a shit.' This became her affirmation, from which arose the concept that if we have all been gifted free will, why would the giver of that free will judge us for however we chose to exercise it? If there is no judgement or punishment from that quarter, why do we keep heaping it on ourselves?

I credit 'The Course' with changing my thinking to living inside out rather than outside in. It introduced to me the concept that when my personality was ruled by an ego empowered by fear, it would continue to tell me that there was something wrong with me. The Course delivered hope as I came to understand the power of my Spiritual self being empowered by love. It led me to understand that it was always my choice which one I gave my power to: love, or fear.

I discovered that the false ideas I held about myself hurt only me. I could no longer deny the pain of the put downs and ridicule. All my moments of fear and untruths were being revealed, not to hurt me any further, but to help me heal. During this time my husband and I parted ways and I credit him for his honesty during our separation process when he commented, 'I could always squash the strong woman when she emerged, but I can no longer.' The parting of ways was like leaving a competition, even though I was unaware I was in one. Despite this, we were able to maintain a harmonious relationship with each other and with our sons. They never had to take sides and we were still able to meet for family celebrations.

Sometimes I felt like I was trapped in a dark tunnel and breaking out of this was as painful as any new birth. Towards the end of the late 1980s and early 1990s, writing poetry became a powerful part of my healing process. Meditating, words would float through my mind and emerge as a poem which best described my state of being in that moment. Frequently the poem would be accompanied by an image that brightly coloured crayons brought to life. I now had words and images to express what was happening, and these helped me stumble towards the light as I began opening to the joy of becoming me.

Hope also became a new companion at this time. This new companion was greatly needed whenever I had a mental temper tantrum, when I desired to halt further growth and return to the bliss of ignorance. To go back to burying all I had sought to avoid was no longer an option for me; the swamp of ignorance in which I had previously lived in was not bliss, and it hurt me.

Continuing my growth required a commitment to embrace my light and my darkness. This was the time to build my own resources. I was learning that the process of embracing the darkness and my shadow self was as necessary as breathing. How else could I find the light of my own truth?

There never was going to be someone to run up to me and tell me about my long-buried truth, that I was pure love and light. It was a journey that only I could take. Only I could discern and discard what didn't support me, and embrace new attitudes towards myself.

My journey to becoming who I am today took me along many roads. These roads included training in many styles of body work and energetic healing techniques. I finally had qualifications, which resulted in my taking another major step and leap of faith into the unknown, at the end of 1988 I began the transition from classroom aide to self-employed therapist and successful businesswoman. I combined both roles for a short period until I eventually developed an income that sustained and supported my lifestyle, one that would finance future training and life choices.

When I could no longer handle an ever-increasing client workload, I took another leap of faith and bought premises and established a clinic, the first of its type in my local area as a centre that brought practitioners and many different types of therapy together.

There were many side trips and detours on my road of becoming me; training to become a voice dialogue practitioner was a notable one. Voice dialogue is based on Carl Jung's 'psychology of selves'. Understanding the whys and interactions of these inner selves in relationship to others gifted me with the awareness to honour all aspects of the voices of my selves. I began the process of healing my inner child and liberating me from the need to search for love and value outside of myself.

During this time of healing and self-discovery, my new husband arrived in my life. He challenged, encouraged, and supported me to continue believing that I could step past my doubts and fears to become the best possible me. He continues to recognise my strengths; he validates and loves both the strong woman and the reclaimed innocent child.

As I look back and reflect on my journey, some of it feels like a story I have read. Each chapter has provided me with many opportunities for growth. In the chapters yet to come I know there will be more challenges, regardless of the spiritual and personal growth I have achieved. I will and still do make mistakes, doubts and fears can still make an appearance, but I have become confident that the life skills I have honed will move me through such moments with love and self-forgiveness to the pure light of my Truth, which cannot be tarnished by self-imposed illusions and which tells me I am good enough, and always have been. I have finally grasped the meaning of the concept 'what I feel I make real', I know the sun is always present even on the darkest of days and blue skies may only be a day away.

Contributing to those new chapters is my writer self, and once again I find myself travelling new landscapes with many new paths and roads to explore. I am not writing to escape the dark tunnel of my previous experience, but to rejoice in the power of stories.

Believe it or not, it was only as I was drawing near to the end of this story that it finally clicked into place that my experience of the Golden Goodness was the moment where my long-held belief in the power of the smile originated.

Then in wonder, a serendipitous moment occurred a few days before committing these final words to paper. I unearthed an I AM statement of affirmation and intent for my future self, written during my rebirthing training course in 1989, which these days is commonly called Breath Work. The folded foolscap paper, handwritten on both sides was creased and yellowed with age and I was filled with the intense delight of discovering the road map that I had drawn up for myself. These sentences especially stood out:

I am now experiencing my own power, love and wisdom. In gratitude I thank the Creator for having created me perfectly. As I develop Spiritually, I open to the light within me. My body can now carry the high potency of my own Holy Spirit. This truth now grows and ripens within me. It is watered by love and nourished by trust.

Unknowingly I had put in place the stepping stones for becoming me and who I am still becoming. I am clearer than ever before that my life is a work of art still in process, and I am the artist.

If I could reach back in time, I would also whisper to my seventeen-year-old self that the time will come when her life will be lived moment by moment, neither stuck in the fear of the past nor the anxiety of the future.

With a smile on my face and joy deep in my heart I rejoice that I am living now.

I have much yet to explore.

Patricia Lovell metaphorically pinches herself to confirm she is not dreaming, and that her inspirational books *Little Bit* and *Willow's Dream* have been published within a year. No-one is more amazed than she. She remains passionate about being of service to others as well as mentoring new and experienced therapists together with creating time to pursue the expression of her voice through the power of the written word.

Patricia continues to visualise a better world for all. A world in which her family and her six grandchildren will know peace and harmony, where the higher good of all is our primary concern. Patricia lives with her husband Brian in the Lake Macquarie area in NSW Australia.

Believe in the magic of your
dreams.
Live each day completely.
For now, beautiful
and the future your treasure.
- Adele Basheer

Forgiveness is one of the most precious gifts we can give ourselves. Forgiveness isn't forgetting the wrongs done to us, or our loved ones, but a reminder that every single one of us are human. To forgive eases the burden of injustice that hangs heavy around our shoulders like a weighted blanket, and allows us to step forward with a light heart ready to embrace all the wonderful opportunities waiting for us. Forgiveness and kindness go hand in hand. With love, compassion, kindness and forgiveness we aren't just gifting ourselves with an incredible life, but all of those around us.

- Mickey Martin

Imperfect
by Toni Lontis

If I ever tell you about my past, it's never because I want you to feel sorry for me, but so that you can understand why I am who I am.

- Unknown

I was born imperfect, BUT I live an utterly extraordinary life, and here's my story of hope and inspiration. *The Colours of Me* version.

I was born in the late 1960s, the first born to young parents living in a rural region of south-west Queensland, Australia. My parents would have been considered average middle class people, well-known and liked across the community. I was born into a well-to-do family, with local connections and support, but with it came family expectations that would cause me pain later in life. It was expected that I would grow up in this rural small town and help out on the farm my parents owned. It was a great start to life.

However, I was also born with a congenital disability, known as a preauricular sinus. This facial defect is present in less than one percent of the population across the world. The result of having this is ongoing major infections and surgery. Before I was two years old, I had had many significant infections. After one of those infections and subsequent surgery I was left with permanent left-sided facial palsy – I could not smile, raise my left eyebrow, my mouth dribbled when I slept, I repeatedly bit the left side of my cheek, and my left eye teared constantly. I looked like I had had a stroke. My earliest memories are of a complete inability to move any part of the left side of my face.

This disability would impact my life in ways I could not have known about, early in my life. I hated being in photos and did not want to smile because I could not make my face work the way I wanted. I did not realise that my reluctance to smile would mean that people saw me as unfriendly and standoffish, unapproachable and rude, none of which was, or is true. It would be decades before I valued myself as a person and understood the special place in the world that I could inhabit by showing up as my imperfect self.

The bullying during school led to very low self-esteem, and that, combined with dysfunctional family life, saw me enter adulthood traumatised, in pain and trying to process life. I proceeded to make decisions that were not in my best interests while looking for love and happiness. From sexual abuse and sexual assault to domestic violence, having a child at twenty-one years of age as an unmarried mother and divorce, all before I was thirty years old. Untreated depression and anxiety bubbled away in the background, threatening to engulf me at any moment. I lived on the edge, petrified that someone would discover how fractured I was.

My first attempt at suicide at fifteen years of age should have been a warning trigger - had I told anyone about it. Subsequent attempts in my twenties also failed to attract the help I needed or to quell the pain I so desperately sought to heal. I was my own worst enemy, refusing to seek help and hiding from the world the pain in my soul. Fear, and fear of judgement, paralysed me. I wish I had known that help was available, I just had to ask. So simple a task but too hard to action at that time in my life.

Imperfect

I arrived in my forties a fractured version of myself, living on the verge of tears and petrified that someone would discover the real me, that I would never find a solution and that I'd die of shame if anyone knew my struggle. All the while diverting attention from myself and functioning at the highest level professionally. I was managing huge portfolios in the Health Department and presenting publicly as strong, capable and dependable.

Then I had a complete nervous breakdown ...

The day started like any other but a small discussion with a work colleague seemed to tip the avalanche of emotions I had, right over the edge. I started crying and could not stop. I had to leave work and after a few days of tears I knew I had to see someone, get some help; I had reached the end of my coping abilities.

My doctor listened to my tearful account of what had happened, asked a few important questions and responded with quiet but firm words. He carefully explained that my brain was exhausted and shutting down, my body was exhausted and saying ENOUGH! His prognosis was dire. I had to STOP work immediately and if I didn't seek to heal and deal with all my trauma, allow myself to get some help and try some medication to soothe my brain, I might not make it to fifty!

I look back on that moment as a turning point in my life, for which I am forever grateful.

Not long after this diagnosis, a chain of events led to my daughter's disclosure regarding sexual abuse at the hands of the man I was to marry, just two weeks before the ceremony. Had I not been at home, starting to heal and on some sort of medication I know that I would not be here to write this story today! From the depths of that deep dark depression and hopelessness, my daughter's disclosure triggered my fight to survive, for her sake.

I decided that I was her mother, and I was placed on this earth to love her unconditionally. While she struggled to heal, I had to heal also so I could be there for her. I knew the statistics, I knew the research around abuse, she had to get through this. I didn't know how hard that would be, didn't realise that there were deeper, darker places to fall.

I did not want to live like this anymore, there had to be more to life, and I wanted to find out what that was. I began a period of ten years struggle, maintaining the semblance of normality while seeking the treatment, medication and therapy that I needed to heal. I researched and read all there was to read about childhood sexual abuse to help my child. I studied, educated myself, and sought a higher level of understanding and consciousness about life, the universe, and my place in it.

The thing about the universe is that as you step towards it and embrace that higher level of understanding, it reaches back and helps you on that journey. By the time I got to my fifties, I had healed a lot of the trauma and retrained my mind to stop the self-destructive thought patterns that had held me back for so long. My daughter had pushed, struggled, and strived to reach her own higher level of healing and understanding. My son grew into a man I am proud of.

As I continued to work hard on myself to be the best person I could be, I stepped away from nursing in clinical practice, Health Department management and moved towards safety and quality auditing and risk assessment. I started my own nurse consultancy company, travelling across Australia, preparing and auditing small hospitals and day surgeries to meet the National Safety and Quality Health Service Standards. It was then, at the height of business success, that I ceased my consultancy work.

You see, as I healed and started to talk a little more about my life to people and friends closer to me, I was encouraged by those I confided in, to write. I let the idea of writing sit with me for a number of years, mulling around in my head, fearful of letting the world know what I had to say. Finally, I made a decision and took action. I sat down to write my book, *Resilience: Memoir of a Broken Little Girl Discovering a Woman of Strength and Beauty* between July 2018 and November 2018.

My memoir was published in January 2019 and, in that year, I decided that I would say yes to any of the opportunities presented to me, without fear. A scary undertaking indeed. The person I was then was still completely introverted, scared to pick up the phone to talk to anyone I didn't know well. I trusted that the universe had a plan, I did not know what that was but I just had to follow where my soul and intuition led.

I embarked on the process of promoting my book, however, I was an author with no real plan, only a newly formulated belief in myself and what I could create. While I was promoting and marketing the book and growing my audiences, I decided to produce the audio version of the book. I would use a voice actress to narrate it for me. Thankfully, I had a producer who quietly and confidently kept encouraging me to narrate the book myself. Finally, I gave in and embarked on the terrifying journey of book narration. I need not have worried, as my producer encouraged and assisted me through the process.

At the end of our long weeks of recording, she commented about my voice's quality and suggested that perhaps I would be great at podcasting. I had a voice that made people want to listen; comforting, calm. In my mind, I thought, 'No way, that's not for me!' But the universe had other plans.

As I grew my social media platforms, I connected with a media company owner in the USA. I asked a few questions about podcasting, to which he replied, 'Have you thought about online radio – streaming audio to the world?' What the heck was online radio? I had never heard of such a thing. I was intrigued, and we set up a Skype call. Little did I know what that conversation would lead to.

The CEO offered me a show of my own under a paid hosting platform. In under a week, Radio Toni was born – my desire to be fearless and give big scary things a go was playing out in real life. From that conversation about one show, a second show was born. I loved live radio, streaming worldwide. I loved the challenge of showing up live on the show and the discipline of maintaining a weekly show at the same time each week, creating content, researching, scheduling, and then I started interviewing people live on air.

I laughingly remember the first six months, I would be physically sick each week before I had to jump behind the microphone. My confidence grew, I started to talk to many unique people from across the planet, and my horizons broadened. I began to wonder what life might look like if this could become a business. Could I enjoy doing what I loved and have it produce an income as well?

That first year was fraught with learning and growing. Seeking to understand just what the universe wanted me to do with these newly acquired talents for interviewing, show coordination and streaming audio. I need not have worried because, towards the end of that first year, I launched 'host your own radio show' packages and started to help others create the type of success that they only dreamed of.

The year 2020 truly shaped my life and business. I feel quite blessed to write this story in 2021 after all the things that transpired in life and in business in 2020. It was a truly incredible, traumatic hell of a year in so many ways.

While COVID-19 has presented many challenges in terms of the business, it has been the family issues that have caused the most growth and boundary setting this year.

In February 2020, I spent a week in Fiji on a 'girls week away' with a stellar group of women. I'm so grateful that I invested in that week, as we have not been able to travel since. The week was filled with spiritual, emotional, and physical healing and rejuvenation, as I let go of many of the limiting thoughts and beliefs I had around success, money, business, impact and vision. I arrived home to my husband's comments, 'I have never seen you look more beautiful; what happened to you over there?' I had never felt better emotionally, physically, or spiritually in my life. I had created a bigger vision and believed that I did not need to know the 'how', that the universe would lead the way.

In many ways, that week away was the biggest blessing of 2020 because had I known what I would come home to, I may have stayed in Fiji just a little longer, and as a travel lover, it was my only getaway for 2020 and probably will be for 2021.

As we all know, COVID-19 created chaos across the world. It led to the cancellation of most of my business plans for 2020, including wonderful retreats to the Philippines, sponsoring feeding and building programs. It also led to the type of family drama I could have done without.

On my arrival home, barely even unpacking, I received the news that my mother was gravely ill. We rushed to the intensive care unit some five hours' drive away, knowing that the previous night my mother had suffered two heart attacks and had been resuscitated twice. Her condition was critical. She was intubated in a semi-coma in the ICU. Fifteen minutes from the hospital, a family member contacted me and suggested that I was not welcome at the hospital. Confused and thinking there had been some mistake, we kept driving, thinking that if I could not see her, at least I would be close if her condition deteriorated.

What transpired on that day and in that waiting room is too painful to write about in this short chapter, but rest assured I will write again when the angst of that time is not so fresh in my mind.

That day I found out that I had been sighted as the causative effect for my mother's heart failure. The sole blame for her condition was dumped at my feet, and I was treated with complete disgust by the family. I'd been accused of daring to write a book about my life that somehow brought the 'family name' into disrepute (all names were changed in the book).

I wrote in a vulnerable, open way about my trauma, dysfunction, mental health challenges and family dysfunction, hoping that it would help others heal and have hope. While I knew my mother wasn't happy with the book, I thought she was supportive. Now my book was being blamed as the stress behind my mother's heart attacks. I was utterly devastated, heartbroken, shattered. That was never my intention and people who know me understand that.

I know that I am not responsible for my mother's health, but the pain of this knowledge sits uncomfortably in my soul, even as I write this chapter today. My rational health and nursing brain know I did not cause this, while my emotional brain struggles to digest the flawed thinking that would cast blame in such a way.

Slowly, I realised that I could no longer have a relationship with my parents and that the time had come to enforce some boundaries in my life; the universe had been quietly showing me this for some years. It was one of the most challenging, most painful things I've had to do, to decide to protect my healing and sanity over the toxic relationships and conversations I had with family members. Their refusal to heal, to let go of expectations, judgment, fear and hatred was and is completely toxic.

So, I shut down all communication with them, and my business and life began to grow and flourish in a way I could never have dreamed it would. Did negativity and toxicity really have such a derogatory impact on my life? I hated knowing this to be true. Dysfunction, judgement, and shame does create negative energy, it does influence you, your energy, and your life path.

Once you start to believe in yourself, your own self-worth, your own purpose, those who don't support you wholeheartedly cannot be part of that path. If you are called to a life purpose that is bigger than yourself, it takes immense courage to stay the course, particularly if those detractors are your own flesh and blood. It leaves hurt in your heart, and pain in your soul to understand that you are NOT responsible for others' healing, you cannot reach them, help them, or heal them past the point where it is dangerous for you to continue to try. You cannot put your own healing in jeopardy to placate those that do not see, those who do not understand, those who will never seek a higher understanding of their own pain. That is ultimately their responsibility, their burden to bear. I had to learn to let go. That letting go broke my heart.

Along this path I also became privy to some astounding family truths that cemented for me the family dysfunction and intergenerational trauma that has plagued the greater family line. I cannot write about this publicly at this stage but hope to one day in the future. I can ensure my own continued healing, learning, and letting go and that of my children and grandchildren.

I am an absolute believer that for evil, judgment, shame, lies and deceit to flourish across humanity, it has to be kept in the dark. That's where evil is perpetuated, that's where judgement takes root, that's where shame dissolves our souls, in the dark secret places where no-one wants to go, where you don't speak, and you don't tell. Shining a light on these concepts and subjects is part of my life now. I know that for evil, judgment and shame to thrive, all it takes is to keep it a secret. Once you shed light on secrets and evil, it ceases to control your life! Light overpowers darkness in all things. Speak your truth, support others that have the courage to do the same. Live life wholeheartedly!

During the time that all this family drama was playing out and as I slowly dealt with the pain of moving away from toxic family relationships, I gained more clarity around where I wanted my life and business to go. Once you open creative space in your life the universe fills it with ideas and concepts to move you forward. This happened for me and I started to see that I could create a business around what I love to do.

All aspects of my life started to align and come together. I was drawn to like-minded people and conversations progressed to working relationships and strategic partnerships. This in turn led to the development of my Collaborative Business Packages to help businesses leverage a global presence using live streaming media. These packages have been a life saver for the business in terms of generating income, we all have to eat and pay mortgages.

The intersection of the development and launch of these income-producing packages changed everything, allowing me to help more people, and in particular, more businesses. The personal and business growth has been an up and down journey but the benefits in terms of human connection, storytelling and shining a light on difficult subjects and topics has been a blessing to be part of. The discovery that you can start a new life trajectory in your fifties is humbling.

I now have multiple shows on multiple platforms with paying clients who invest their time with me and my business to show them how to leverage a digital presence across the world. It is a privilege for me to co-host with these business leaders and spread the messages they have. In January 2021, I launched my own channel on BINGE networks in the USA and worldwide, with a potential 209 million viewers.

So, wonderful readers, just by showing up as my imperfect self, daring to believe in me, and creating the right mindset with education and action-taking, I aim to continue to change the world in my own small way. Everyone has a story, everyone has something to say, and I want to help you say it. I want to inspire, empower, educate, and help the world one show at a time.

Here's my future vision.

'I want to provide an opportunity for all those that have the courage to rise above their trauma, to actualise their dreams denied to them by injustice.'
Toni Lontis 2021

Toni Lontis was a nurse for thirty-five years across many specialties and levels of heath. In 2018 Toni wrote about her life, after being encouraged to do so during her healing and self-discovery processes. *Resilience - Memoir of a Broken Little Girl discovering a Woman of Strength and Beauty* was published in January 2019.

Toni then embarked on a marketing strategy, increasing her social media presence and creating networks. She now has multiple live streaming TV radio shows on different platforms broadcasting to the world, including her own channel on BINGE Networks. She uses the power of the spoken word to tell the stories that the world needs to hear.

Sometimes when you are in a dark place, you think you've been buried, but actually you've been planted.
— The Stencil Smith

A PIVOT
It hit me unexpectedly
Couldn't finish the meal
I was overcome
By a tightness in my chest
Gasping
I collapsed onto the dark walnut floor
Its unexpected coolness alerted me
Its growing warmth cradled my eyes
The last thing I saw was a layer of dust
In front of my nose
I need to Swiffer, I thought
The scent of dry rosemary crust
Filled my nostrils
Whiffs of a stale meal
The moist turkey a distant memory
It had barely been five minutes
Although I could not be sure
I was only able to count
My beating heart pounding in my ear
I succumbed to the gentle lullaby
Of oblivion

A Pivot
by Sonee Singh

I had been in my new house outside of Seattle for barely a month. I had unpacked, decorated, and was just beginning to gain a sense of belonging in my home. Suddenly, I got sick. One moment I was eating Thanksgiving leftovers and the next I couldn't get up.

I ended up in the hospital with a fully collapsed right lung and a partially collapsed left lung due to a sudden onset of aggressive pneumonia. The doctors didn't understand how I could breathe, and after several weeks in the hospital, they were not able to determine the cause. It took me months to recover. I ended up with liver failure because I had been doused with so many drugs.

I recovered. I regained function in my lungs and in my liver. My hair grew back – partially – after I lost clumps of it. I regained strength – enough to hike to the Tiger's Nest temple in Bhutan several months later. I gained my weight back, to my dismay – the one thing I didn't want to come back.

I knew the experience was meant to wake me up somehow. Health had often been an indicator that I needed to do things differently. Headaches, migraines, allergies, hypothyroidism, rashes, asthma and dysmenorrhea had been signs that I needed to stop, quiet my thoughts, still my actions, change my approach and shift my perception. Sometimes I listened and other times I didn't. When I got sick with pneumonia I very much wanted to listen. I knew I needed a new direction; a new horizon to gaze upon; a new way to live. But I didn't know where to turn. It was a true halting.

I was confused by the halt because I had already started a personal revolution of sorts. For most of my life, I had felt the push for perfection and succumbed to it. I knew how to be efficient, how to be productive, and how to be dependable. I knew how to do things well. In doing so, I had pursued a career that didn't fulfil me. It seemed more important to be good at something than it was to find it fulfilling. It turned out, in that push for perfection, I had forgotten to seek true joy.

For many years I wasn't aware of this. It was only when people said to me:

'You have such an analytical approach.'

Or, 'You're the spreadsheet queen.'

Or, 'You are so passionate about what you do.'

None of it was a lie. Passion may have been a push, but did I enjoy what I did? I was the person they came to for problem solving or for training. Still, the comments didn't fit me. I would wonder, 'Is there more than this?'

I had identified that something needed to shift; I needed to gain purpose. I yearned to do something that brought meaning to my life. More importantly, I yearned to do something that made me feel meaningful.

I thought that pursuing my entrepreneurial spirit would bring me what I was seeking. Three years before my illness, I left a career in hospitality to go back to school and start my own business. I became a wellness coach and produced custom-made aromatherapy products.

As I started to recover from the pneumonia, I realised my business didn't fill my heart the way it had before getting sick. I continued what I was doing, but I did so listlessly. It was clear that I didn't want to be where I was – physically, mentally, and spiritually. I regained health and strength in my body, but not in my soul.

It turned out that my revolution wasn't deep enough. I had waded up to my knees into the waters of change, but I needed to plunge all the way in, to hold my breath underwater, and to emerge only after the water had seeped into my bones. Deep down I knew that all along, I had long felt my true calling, but I didn't know if I had it in me to pursue it.

I know many a terrible driver
Ones who don't think they are
Despite regularly missing stop signs
Not properly checking if a car is coming
Repeatedly driving over dividers and sidewalks
Constantly missing turns

I claim to be a good driver
Perhaps I'm too careful
Some say I check too much
Constantly turning my head
Others that I drive like a true Amazon
Zigzagging from one lane to another

I feel more comfortable behind the wheel
Than I do in other areas in my life
An immense sense of calm floods me
A security I don't feel in other places
A sense of freedom and certainty
A love for the wonder of the road

The excitement of what the trip will bring
The sceneries to delight upon
If only I could extend that sense of trust
Hold on to the wheel of life
Guide my own with the same level of confidence
Sense of safety and self-assuredness

I have wanted to be a writer since I was a child, and although the thought re-emerged throughout the years, I didn't pursue it with seriousness. I wrote stories but I didn't tell anyone. That's not true. I told a boss once during a performance review. He asked me to share a personal goal and I couldn't think of anything else to say. But he didn't know the significance of these stories. Nor did anyone else.

Dedicating myself to writing full-time didn't seem like an option. I did not believe I was any good or that I could make a living from it. It seemed like such a large impossibility that I gave up on the dream.

Yet it surrounded me. In every position I held throughout my career, I did some form of writing. It wasn't the type of writing I wanted to be doing, but it was always the aspect of my job that I enjoyed the most. Even as part of my coaching business, I wrote weekly health-related articles that I posted on my website. I couldn't write while I was in the hospital, but while I was recovering at home it became my favourite task. It challenged me sufficiently to want to improve my writing and to provide more value to my readers.

The universe responded. I came across a writing course offered by *Elephant Journal* called Elephant Academy. I jumped at the opportunity and joined. The lessons became my focus and I prioritised writing my articles over other tasks. My writing improved. I gained the courage to submit articles to trade publications and I got them published. I also published a few pieces in *Elephant Journal*.

This opened me up to want to do more, and I wanted to push myself further. The universe once again delivered. I came across a writing challenge promising to reignite inspiration. Joanne Fedler provided writing prompts every day for a week. I marvelled at what emerged when I had no agenda to write about, and so when Joanne offered an Author Awakening Adventure to share her guidance on how to find a writing voice, once again, I did not hesitate.

> *I did eventually find it*
> *That sense of safety*
> *And self-assuredness*
> *When I write*
> *I embark on a journey*
> *I don't know the destination*
> *Or what I will encounter along the way*
> *I feel an openness like no other*

Elephant Journal's writing academy had another unintended consequence. I discovered a joy in having a community of like-minded writers. The bond was such that a group of us created a Facebook group in which we read Julia Cameron's *The Artist's Way*, sharing our thoughts as we moved through each chapter.

I started my own version of morning pages, an exercise Cameron suggests we undertake to tap into our creative potential. It involves handwriting non-stop until three notebook pages are filled. Julia suggests doing this first thing in the morning to best access our subconscious. I couldn't write first thing in the morning, but I did start writing every day.

Some of the pages were pure gibberish, especially at first, but I didn't care. My mind gradually grew to feel at peace. I reignited my meditation practice and eventually, it merged with my writing. The cacophony that filled my thoughts stilled, leaving me with moments of unexpected quiet.

Unbeknownst to me, my life began to shift. I released my subconscious onto the page. I discovered parts of myself I didn't know were there and uncovered aspects of myself I had long forgotten. I saw magic appear on the page. Words came out that I didn't know I had in me. I found a form of self-expression and an outlet I didn't realise was available to me.

I felt unburdened. No-one would ever have to see what I wrote and that gave me the freedom to say anything at all. To make sure of it, I threw the pages into a recycling bin. It would have been more dramatic to burn the notebooks, but I was afraid of unleashing an uncontrollable fire.

Julia Cameron states that one of the benefits of morning pages is to connect with our intuition. I hadn't yet managed to do that in my writing. It felt like a distant goal, yet something in me said that tapping into my intuition would help me to find myself and to propel myself in my quest for meaning. I yearned for it having heard so many people tell me that you never go wrong when you listen to your intuition. I knew intuition was linked to gut feeling. I recognised that it felt scary to act on instinct because I was giving in to an impulse without knowing the result. I also knew that when I ignored my gut, I paid the price. I wanted to stop going wrong, to stop making mistakes, and to stop ignoring my inner voice.

I flew into New York ten months after becoming ill and walked to Central Park with a notebook in my hand. I chose a rock to sit on to meditate. I wrote in my notebook for a while but felt called to sit in silence. I sat in the park, put my hands on my heart and set an intention to know what it felt like to connect with my intuition.

As I grew quiet, I focused on sending my breath in and out of my heart centre. After a few minutes, I felt a transcendent sense of peace.

For the first time in my life, I felt a surrender, and in that absolute release, I heard a voice.

'Go,' it said.

I didn't know where the voice came from. It sounded like it was within my head and it sort of sounded like my own voice, but it wasn't me. There was a different quality to it; it had a confidence I didn't have.

'Go where?' I asked, in my head.

And it told me. I had been debating on whether to book a trip, and somehow, this voice knew that I had been pondering the question.

'How do I heal myself?' I asked, although what I really wanted to know was how do I feel whole, how do I make sure that I matter, what is my life's purpose, and why am I here? But I didn't want to scare the voice away, so I kept to the one question.

'Love yourself,' it said.

It sounded simple, yet monumental. I now know it is hard to love yourself when you have been your own last priority, but I didn't know that back then. I wondered what I needed to do. Did that mean I had to love my gnarly feet? The stubborn fat on my body? Did that mean I needed to love myself when I stayed quiet, knowing I should speak up? Did that mean I needed to love every outburst I had? Every time I hurt someone? Every time I hurt myself? Every time I felt small?

I started with little things. It was easiest to love and appreciate the details: my hands, my manicured toenails, my smile. Then, I listed qualities: my sense of responsibility, my ability to listen, and so on, because I didn't know how else to start on this journey of self-love.

I felt an opening that day. I was able to tap into my feelings in a way I hadn't been able to before. I felt better; lighter. I returned to Seattle with a renewed perspective.

I came to learn that my purpose was not a job, a career, or a profession, as I once had thought. I realised that it didn't matter what I became, what title I had, or what I 'did' with my life. As long as I was happy, I was fulfilling my purpose. When I was happy, others around me could be happy as well, as happiness spreads.

I shared this with someone who asked, 'What if killing others makes you happy?'

I don't believe it is possible to feel true happiness by inflicting pain upon another – that is about power and control because it is at the cost of another.

True happiness is in no way dependent on another. True happiness doesn't infringe upon others or take away from them. True happiness is for the highest good of all. True happiness comes from within. The Gospel of Thomas states, 'If you bring forth what is within you, what you bring forth will save you. If you do not bring forth what is within you, what you do not bring forth will destroy you.'

I put more effort into writing, and it became the most liberating of experiences, revealing the secrets I kept hidden – even from myself. I released the stories that were entrenched in me and those shrouded in secrecy. I expressed despair and loneliness as I let it go. In its stead, I discovered a fascination for the ethereal. It is in writing that I discovered what it meant to be truly free.

> *I pulled on every last finger*
> *Planted my shoulders firmly*
> *Squishing my knees into the soil*
> *Allowed my hips to reach Mother in the earth*
> *Reached my elbows in the wind*
> *Allowed my hairs to extend to Father in the sky*
> *A beautiful union erupted in my spirit*
> *An so it came to be*
> *Letter by letter*
> *Word by word*

I found the shape of me
The voice I didn't know I had
The ease I didn't know I had
The confidence I didn't know I had
The vitality I didn't know I had
I felt a brightness so elating
I filled the space
With all of me

I have moved a lot in my life, feeling more at home in the wind than in places where I lived. I have felt I am in an eternal holding pattern. Whenever I arrived at a new place, I waited for signs to tell me it was time to pack up. Sometimes I didn't give a place a chance. At other times, I adapted easily, but the thought in the back of my mind that was prepared to move on, never left. I remained detached sufficiently so I wouldn't grow roots, so that I made sure I didn't belong; and so that the place didn't take hold of me.

My sense of belonging came from my habits; the practices that I kept. What mattered was that I kept these habits with me. Writing started like an adventure, and without having conscious awareness, it became my home. I started realising that, as I let go of my previous life, I could be anywhere. It didn't matter where I was and how long I stayed.

Writing made me recognise why I was in search for meaning. I had spent my life doing what I thought others wanted me to do. I had spent my life doing what I was good at, but not what I wanted to do. I had spent my life portraying an image that wasn't me, and I had done it for so long, I had lost myself.

I felt compelled to put pen to paper or finger to keyboard. I did both and it didn't matter how the writing came as long as it did; my hands needed to remain in motion. Whether what emerged was fiction or non-fiction was irrelevant. What mattered was that I found a form of connection: a connection to myself, to God, to the universe, to my past, to my present, to my future, to the dead and to the living. Through that connection I found freedom; a freedom of expression that allowed me to be me. In doing, I made space for others to be themselves, and collectively for all of us to recognise we are a part of each other.

All this happened in 2017. Looking back on it, I realise that the series of events resulted in one of the greatest pivots of my life. I've had others, but this one was particularly transformative. When I revisit the moment it all began, I can see how ill health was my call to action. The illness I experienced was a type of stepping stone, a part of my awakening to discover parts of myself that I had kept hidden because I had not truly given myself a chance. It was no surprise that as the universe threw writing in my path, I rediscovered that eight-year-old girl and healed her into a mature woman who conceded her path to being herself.

The pneumonia was a call to action and my healing happened in layers. One layer involved opening to the messages from the universe. Back then, I assumed the events that unfolded were mere coincidences, but I soon recognised the universe was responding to me. The more I asked, the more it gave. It even gave me things I didn't know I wanted – or needed.

The other layer was reclaiming myself by honouring the strings in my heart. As I jumped at opportunities that presented themselves, I realised that, truly, I was following what I had within. Through that process, I figured out what I needed to be myself. Writing guided me, healed me, and moulded itself into who I am.

The third layer was opening up to my intuition so that I could listen to my inner voice and see how it – and I – were connected to the calling of the universe. Through my intuition, the two callings – those of my heart and the universe – become one.

I was forced to heal. In that healing I found surrender. The more I surrendered, the less I did, and the more peace I felt. The key was giving up, but not in defeat. The giving up was in control. In giving up control I opened myself to what I held within and to what the world had to provide. I feel more myself now than I have ever felt before.

I am still playing the game of self-love. I know it extends far beyond the little things – although, they help. I have befriended the voice in my head. I have regular conversations with it, and I know it is the sound of my intuition, a pathway for me to connect with myself, and a way for me to listen to the wisdom of the universe. In doing so, I honour myself. For now, I have found that to be the best form of self-love.

I am brave enough to step forward
I love myself
I lead my life with great vision
I trust the messages I receive in my heart.

Sonee Singh is a cross-cultural seeker of deep knowing. Her tales are of her character's definitive moments on their life's journey. The mystical and spiritual are integral in her storytelling, as is her multi-cultural background.

Sonee is of Indian descent, born in Mexico, raised in Colombia, and now, resident in the United States. When not travelling, reading, or writing, she indulges in meditation, yoga and aromatherapy. She holds a Bachelor of Arts in Biology and Society and a Master of Management in Hospitality from Cornell University, and a Master of Science in Complementary Alternative Medicine from American College of Healthcare Sciences.

Letter from 'The Lucky One'

by Lindy Wyse

*D*earest Mom,

    I lost you in the midst of the COVID-19 lockdown. Your heartbreaking and arduous battle with Alzheimer's concluded, you leave a vacuous, unfillable void. I always felt that nobody in the world was meant to be my Mommy and if I could have chosen my mother from heaven's garden, I would have picked you. I am so happy that I told you this before you 'lost your marbles!!' You teared up. 'Dust in my eyes,' you said. In your passing, it comforts me to talk to you as if you were still here – a lifelong habit of wanting to share everything with you.

    As I am called to reflect on how my unique human experiences have shaped me, it makes perfect sense to do so in a letter to you. I lament the missed opportunities to discuss our shared trauma, post-traumatic stress disorder (PTSD) and how it shaped our lives. I feel the need now more than ever to have this important dialogue, resting the weariness of my soul in the lightness of your own, where I always sought sanctuary through your unconditional love and infinite faith in me. So, where do I start, Ma? On reflection, there are three main shared traumas that impacted our lives. We've walked through fire together, but you've carried me most of the way.

The Drowning

It was a winter morning in Matabeleland (Zimbabwe's southern-most province) in 1976 and the five of us had woken up from a stopover at the Gwaai River Hotel, a halfway house between our home town of Wankie and Bulawayo, the capital city of Matabeleland.

In your words, 'Dad was having a bath and I was packing to go. I had asked Graham to look after you while I packed. Mike sauntered into the room in a daydream, just as I had a funny feeling. I said to him: 'Please go and check on Lindy.' As he left the room, I yelled: 'Run!' At this point, Dad was getting out of the bath. Mike came tearing back into the room, screaming: 'Lindy's in the pool!' Dad shot out of the bathroom in a dressing gown that was too short for him, showing off his bum, but he didn't care! I remember arriving at the pool, seeing you lying face down and motionless. It was the worst moment of my life.'

Mom, I can still see your face and hear your voice when you said, 'I know it sounds crazy, but I know that you died. I prayed with all my heart and you came back to me. You are so lucky to be alive and we are so lucky to have you.' Mommy, these words have stuck with me my whole life and make me feel so grateful to be on this earth, despite the turbulence. Having been face down in the water for ten minutes, I was given mouth-to-mouth resuscitation for fifteen minutes by a fellow hotel guest, Mrs Pixie Phillips. At the age of eight, I got to thank her for saving my life. When I feel suffocated by life's pressures, I remember: I was meant to overcome; I simply was meant to still be here.

The Attack

I was three and it was turbulent times in Rhodesia, three years before the transition to Zimbabwean independence. It was 1977, the Rhodesian

Letter From the 'Lucky One'

Bush War had escalated and we were caught in the crossfire. I remember taking cover in the middle of the night, in the bunker of our house, with you, Graham and Mike. We all lay flat on our tummies, the sky all lit up outside, listening to the sounds of gunfire and grenades. Dad wasn't there. He worked in the Government's administrative arm as the region's District Commissioner. On realising he'd been at the pub, you were furious! The sky was so pretty. What was all the fuss about? 'Poop, get down!' you pleaded, pulling my arm and covering me, so I wouldn't toddle off again. You had three of us to keep calm and I managed to wriggle free, pacing up and down, saying: 'In the deep freeze, I've got strawberry ice cream, vanilla ice cream and chocolate ice cream.' Although calm on the night, and clearly grateful for my blessings, the trauma impacted my toddler brain. Prior to the incident, I was not afraid of thunderstorms. Following the incident, every time there was a storm, I flew under my bed, absolutely terrified, thinking our house was under attack.

Oh Mommy, how brave you were, raising children in the middle of a bush war! To do the monthly grocery shopping, you would travel nonchalantly and elegantly, in an armoured vehicle convoy, dressed impeccably with matching handbag and shoes, and a semiautomatic weapon lying across your lap. I often think of you, now that I am faced with my own challenges of parenting two beautiful children with vast and varied intricacies. I remind myself that if you could cope, then so can I. You soldiered on, with so much love and laughter, despite your own undiagnosed PTSD. What an inspiration.

The Accident

There is the me before the accident, and the me after. Today, I hardly ever talk about it, but what happened that day, Mom, and the time that followed, forever altered me. It was 1994, I had left school and was working in Harare, saving for my ticket to London, my passage to adventure. We'd been at Sonia Hill's kitchen tea, her wedding two weeks away. I offered to drive home in our small farm truck. I was a new, but cautious driver, so you accepted. I proceeded after a few minutes, onto the main tarred road, leading us home to the farm. In a few surreal seconds, with you by my side, time simultaneously stood still and vanished. An elderly man stepped into the road, metres away from us. I had no time or means to avoid an impact. Either way I swerved he would move in the same direction. He collided with our car, his right hip hitting the front grill, and was thrown into the air, coming down on the left side of his forehead, colliding with the windscreen. I felt nauseous, and it was as if my whole psyche was hovering in a vortex above my body, quietly observing the scene. I was nineteen. Time slipped into fast forward as I pulled over, rushing to the man's side, squeezing his hand, saying over and over again, 'I'm so sorry!' Within minutes we had a crowd, and somebody fetched a policeman.

I gave my statement, with Dad by my side, assuring the policeman on duty that I had been travelling under the speed limit and that I had done everything I could to avoid hitting this man. He assured me that according to his calculations, it did not appear likely that I had been speeding. The finer details of the events were blanketed in a hazy shroud of shock, but I remember feeling mortified that I was unable to tell this old man, in his own language, how sorry I was for what had happened. I loved the land and the people, yet how could I have been so callously remiss as to not commit to learning the language enough to communicate my deep, deep remorse at what had just occurred?

I feel contrition, too, for not memorising his name. It was an act of self-preservation, as to put a name to this man was simply too confronting; too real. I later named him 'Enos', and I remember him being taken away in an ambulance, destined for Harare. I had made plans to see some friends that night, but I really didn't feel like going. Being a 'people pleaser', I went, regrettably, enduring flippant comments from

Letter From the 'Lucky One'

acquaintances that down-played the seriousness of the incident. I was young, confused and terrified, but I scolded myself: 'What kind of person are you, to not stand up to that mindset?!' There were no mobile phones in those days, just 'party lines' and 'bush telegraph'. When I returned to the farm the next day, you and Dad were both waiting to greet me. I got out of the car. Looking at Dad, then at you, Mom, and searching the crumples of your sorrowful face for your kind brown eyes, I knew: 'Enos' was dead.

In the days following the accident, I clearly remember Dad saying: 'This will never leave you.' I knew he was right, Mommy. Within two weeks, I attended Sonia and Ivan's wedding in Harare; a joyous and jovial affair, with the whole of our farming community present, the atmosphere abuzz with the cacophony of convivial laughter, kaleidoscopic outfits and large, colourful personalities. I was permitted a partner, so naturally I brought the inimitable Gary along (my best mate and your favourite of all my male friends). 'Why don't you go out with him? He's loooovely!' you'd say. 'I don't want to ruin our friendship,' I'd retort. I remember how you cried (as you did at our wedding) when I told you, four years later over the phone from London, that we were finally a couple. Whilst at Sonia's wedding, I went through the motions, but I felt that I had no right to have fun, be cheery or indeed be happy ever again. Devastated that I had been responsible for the ending of a human life, I didn't know how or why life should ever go back to normal; that 'normal' no longer existed. It was such an indescribably heavy feeling that only abated at night when I sobbed some of the pain away. However, just when I felt that the situation could not be more dire, I was dealt a heavy blow.

The police inspector summoned me to the station. With Dad by my side, I was advised that my statement, together with three witness statements, had been examined. I was issued with a charge of 'Culpable Homicide' (under Zimbabwean law, the definition was 'murder without intent'). I was to present to the Magistrates' Court within three months to take the stand.

The smell of the police station was nauseating; a rancid smell of unwashed bodies mixed with the scent of paper, floor polish and cheap cologne. Doing my damnedest to hold my body and brain in check, I asked what my punishment would be, if found guilty. The inspector advised me that I would likely face five years imprisonment.

My court date arrived and I was a mess, as were you and Dad. You helped me choose some smart clothes and held my hand, occasionally stroking my hair, all the way to the courthouse, as we bumped away in a borrowed truck. Dad was driving and Arnold, our farm manager, was sitting in the back. He came to assist by translating anything we didn't understand during the proceedings.

The judge was a sombre, formidable looking man of medium height and solid build, made all the more forboding by his flowy, black gown. I looked intently at the man who was to ultimately decide my fate and deliver my verdict. I just had to trust that he would be unbiased. Everybody who needed to be there was on time. The one exception was my lawyer, a thin, chaotic man, provided to the family by our car insurance company. He was so different to the usual stereotypical suave lawyer persona. He drove an old yellow car with papers strewn all over the back seat and wore a baggy, crumpled suit. We'd only met once, and I worried about the strength of his case. Bustling towards us, in a swirl of chaos and nervous energy, he gave me a kind smile and said, 'Shall we?' I hugged you and Dad, thanked Arnold and walked in with 'Captain Chaos'. You, Dad and Arnold sat behind me. The proceedings began.

One by one, the witnesses stood in the stand, testifying against me, including the police officer who chose to speak in Shona, which although I couldn't speak it, I understood it very well. Dismayed as I realised that he, too, was professing my guilt, along with the others, I suddenly felt sick and sure that I was doomed to enduring the unthinkable consequences of a jail sentence. As I took the stand, I was intent on speaking clearly and calmly. With hands and voice shaking, I slowly retold every detail of the accident, choosing every word as carefully as I could. The lawyer for the state spoke in English, stating that my reckless driving resulted in the fate of the deceased.

When 'Captain Chaos' finally spoke, I was taken by surprise. His delivery was superb! He questioned how one witness could have seen the accident, given his position in his home near the road at the time; he examined the sobriety and presence of the other witness and challenged the policeman's mathematical skills. The judge was meant to remain ambivalent, but I could sense he was clearly entertained.

The court adjourned for recess and it was during this break that I approached a lady who had been crying. From what I understood, she was the niece of Enos. I told her, with Arnold's help, that I was so very sorry about what had happened. Unsmiling, she nodded her understanding and seemed to appreciate my words. I was later told that she approached Dad (via Arnold) and asked for some money for food and beer, or for Dad to donate a cow. I knew that Shona burials were different to what was customary in my own family, but I didn't fully understand the request, as Enos had already been buried. I later learned that she was asking for donations towards the *bira* or *kurova guva,* a lengthy traditional mourning ceremony held a year later by family and friends, at a person's *kumusha* – their homeland. It is a settling of the spirit ceremony, a time after the rains have sunk into the burial site and the earth has truly settled, when the spirit may now come home.

It is with deep regret that I did not fully understand the importance of this. To contribute to the *bira* would have been the right thing to do for Enos and his family, and it would have given me immense peace to know that I had helped in this way. However, Dad would not compromise my chances in any form and declined the request, believing that to agree would appear to some as an admission of guilt.

After a twenty-minute interval, we walked back inside to hear the judge's verdict. Before delivering it, the judge saw fit to pull the State lawyer's case to shreds, causing a twitter of amusement. He now seemed less imposing, and a flicker of hope filled my heart, which suddenly felt lighter than it had in months.

'Can you not see that this was clearly an accident whereby the young driver and her mother, the passenger, were clearly and simply in the wrong place at the wrong time? The pedestrian looked left but not right before crossing the road making it impossible to avoid an impact. May the State prosecutor please exercise due diligence in future cases by not wasting the State's time and resources in such cut and dry cases. I hereby deliver the verdict: Not Guilty. Case dismissed.'

Mommy, your face was a scrunched-up picture of love and relief and I took solace in your embrace, gently sobbing out my relief in the warm crook of your shoulder. The heaviness eased with each passing day, however, the guilt remained, festering and bubbling away. Although I spoke in length with the spirit of Enos, telling him how sorry I was, it would only be decades later in Brisbane that I would truly feel the presence of his spirit telling me, 'You must let this go now. It was an accident. My spirit is at peace. I am home.'

What followed was intense self-reflection and I called my character into close examination, questioning who I wanted to be in my life and the answer was simple: kind without prejudice. This later developed into two values by which I determine to live my life: Service and Growth. These two values go hand in hand; you cannot truly serve if you do not embrace personal growth.

Letter From the 'Lucky One'

The accident had triggered a deep discomfort within, and in my worst moments, a self-loathing, pulling me into a deep depression. Whilst still in Zimbabwe until 1996, I leaned on the love and support of my family and friends. Mental health was very much a taboo subject and counselling was not yet mainstream. The emotional pain became so heavy by the time I got to the UK that whilst living and working in a hunting lodge in Scotland, I tried to access the gun cabinet, to end it all. My depression led me to some questionable decisions, and at the time I had recently exited an abusive relationship which had cemented my suspicions: my life was not of value. The code to the cabinet had been changed. I lay on the floor and sobbed, and as I did so, I felt my body and soul ensconced with unconditional love and light, and the words came to my mind: 'You are so lucky to be here, and we are so lucky to have you.' I knew I needed to go home.

After a wonderful reunion with my *kumusha,* I felt restored and returned to London. I made new friends, connected with old ones, including Gary, who by this time was living on the outskirts. Before too long, we were dating, and although he didn't fully understand my depression, he simply loved me through it. Having match-made two dear friends five years previously, I returned to Zimbabwe a year later to be maid of honour at their wedding. They would later join us in London in May 2000, survivors of political violence in Zimbabwe. As you know, Mommy, those were dark times indeed when Robert Mugabe tightened his power grip. Our beloved farm was seized by the government, but you and Dad are survivors, so you took refuge in South Africa, before moving to New Zealand in 2010, to be closer to your kids.

The years I was living in London between 2000 and 2008 (before Gary and I moved to Brisbane), hold such happy memories. I discovered the restorative power of friendship and love, as well as the healing power of laughter, for how we laughed! We continue to do so today, climbing uphill with our beautiful, complex children, but hand in hand, pulling each other along, striving for the next pinnacle ahead. Your joint legacy with Dad – that of love and laughter – inspired me to secure a life partner with whom I could laugh, for you both taught me the true value of always seeking out the lightness in any situation and the healing power of laughter and unconditional love.

Ma, although you and I have endured multiple shared and individual traumas, leading both of us to parent out of a place of hypervigilance, we have always laughed through it all. Our experiences have also served us well, making us both very instinctive and intuitive Mama Bears. In 2015, Mommy, your Alzheimer's had progressed significantly, whilst I was struggling to cope with two children with undiagnosed issues, on top of past traumas. How I missed you so – more than ever before! Motherhood was the proverbial 'last straw' that broke this little camel's back. I was diagnosed with Graves' disease, an autoimmune disorder. I became very ill.

Gary was very supportive and advised me to give myself time and space to heal. It was during the year I took off from work that I was diagnosed with PTSD. I underwent counselling and commenced medication for anxiety and depression. I reframed destructive inner thoughts, changing the most recurring thought: 'I can't do this,' to 'How can I do this?' The best way I could cope was by throwing unconditional love at myself and my family. I started finding medical answers to the complexities of my children and discovered multiple pathways to healing: running, meditating, drawing and writing. I learned that in Chinese medicine, Graves' Disease represents a lack of self-expression, so I wrote thank you letters to all my traumas, thanking them for what they had taught me, which came down to one thing: an immense gratitude for life, exactly as it is. I have not stopped writing since. My healing was consolidated when I again spoke to the spirit of Enos and felt with all my heart that he was telling me to let it all go.

It is fast-approaching one year since we lost you in COVID-19. It is looking likely that soon we will be able to freely travel to New Zealand. Mike and I are coming soon, Mommy. We will join Dad and Grat for your *bira*, your 'settling of spirit'. As I think of this, I am filled with deep gratitude for the way you loved me: with laughter, presence, gratitude, and acceptance. You loved me exactly the way I was: broken and put back together, my edges catching the light, casting both rainbows and shadow. Your unconditional love was the earth from which I blossomed, unfurling and blooming into my unique shades and hues. To honour you I will endeavour to live by your words, 'You are so lucky to be here, and we are so lucky to have you.' When I was little, I was called 'Lindiwe', the Ndebele version of my name, meaning 'the one who has been waited for'. I will continue to attempt to live my life worthy of this name. I am in my heart and mind and will always be 'Nhlahla - The Lucky One'.

With so much gratitude, your ever-loving,
Poop (Lindiwe Nhlahla!) xxx

Lindy Wyse was born and bred in Zimbabwe. She is an author and illustrator with a passion for creatively teaching life skills to kids. Drawing on her experiences working in the disability and mental health sectors, as well as through her own experiences of overcoming trauma, Lindy believes in the healing power of words and the resilience of the human spirit. Lindy is fascinated by our capacity for transformation.

Tinker Tailor's Toolbox (For Mending Broken Hearts) is Lindy's first children's book, published in 2020, under the name Lindy Jelliman. She is also a contributing poet in the anthology *Globalisation: The Sphere Keeps Spinning* (MMH Press, 2021). Lindy lives in Brisbane with her husband and two kids.

When Demons Breathe New Perspective

by Rachel Francis

There was a metronome which I embedded in a rational corner of my subconscious. I used its continuous rhythm as a comfort during times of extreme emotional, psychological, or physical tension. For me, the simple 'tick … tick … tick …', the regular tempo of the pendulum was a massive stress-reducing tool, which I controlled. Through its rigid regular cadence, I refocused and broke the circuit of negativity which otherwise could have become obsessively overwhelming. This metronome fed on misery and would only stop when the particular power source was completely abated, allowing my more positive internal dialogue to take over. It was a friend, disrupting my state of panic and taking my awareness to a level closer to serenity, enabling the growth of perspective.

I am under no illusions and understand fully that this was an autodidactic coping mechanism that allowed me to influence the path of my raw emotional state, redirecting my response towards the logical. The greater the stress, the louder I allowed the beat of the metronome to pulse. The internal sound took me out of the moment, enabled me to calm my breathing and gave me time to centre my approach or reaction.

Immediately on sensing that a particular anxiety had infiltrated, I invested time in this metronome process. Once I regained a certain mental clarity within the situation, I asked myself, 'What in this present situation can I control?' and, 'How do I control that element?' This creative approach worked, but didn't always work smoothly; it was something I retaught myself over many years in an effort to reframe anxiety.

On Friday 7 October 2016, the walls (which began to close in on me many months before) collapsed, burying me in my own catastrophic panic. The metronome played incessantly at its loudest. The words we had expected were said, and they could not be unsaid. My absolute dread was now a clear and present reality. The innocent, comfortable planned-out world I had created was now irrelevant as my life direction exploded onto an alternative course. My burning desire to 'get off this new merry-go-round' was immaterial. Eight words spoken by one particular individual with an absolute level of confidence destroyed my soul, and I disappeared.

April 2017 Social Media post:

> One of the toughest conversations any parent will have to have with their child involves the sentence, 'Mom has breast cancer.' The year 2016 was pretty shit for many, the foremost in my world being that I was diagnosed with breast cancer. Simon and I have faced the anxiety, fear, dread and stress that these words and this disease bring. Breast cancer is horrendous, every element of it. It is a disease that does not discriminate, is not prejudice, it has no concern for who you are or what your plans are for the future. Although I am not yet finished my treatment or surgeries, and I will not officially be 'discharged' from the various medical services/hospital departments until early 2022, there is a confidence that I am currently cancer free.
>
> The reason for this, my most personal of public social media

posts, is not to install or generate fear, grief, pity or sorrow in you – there are enough of these demons tormenting me. Instead, it is to ask two things of you please:

1) Go and have whatever cancer screening is appropriate for you and have regular screening. My breast cancer was not a lump and there was no physical pain (initially). It was only discovered through screening.

2) Open dialogue and encourage those who are important to you, to undertake regular cancer screening.

I have been told countless times that we are lucky my breast cancer was found early – of this I am convinced. I have been told that as a result of the hellish decisions Simon and I were forced to make because of this diagnosis, I now have a better chance of seeing my son enter primary school. Cancer is not a pleasant disease in any way, but please, if you are to be cursed as I have been, if you are forced to have a similar conversation with your child or loved ones, give yourself every possible opportunity to beat the f*cker and don't put off screening.

My breast cancer journey was made extensively easier as a result of the love, optimism, support and positivity of those around me – that is what gave me my strength.

The eight most impactful words spoken by my consultant were, 'I don't have good news for you Rachel,' which she swiftly followed with, 'but we have a plan.' Tick … tick … tick … Sadly, the damage was done and although I chose to focus on the latter half of her introduction, the demons had laid siege to my being and their truth hurt. Anarchy established itself, firmly corrupting my thought process. The rest of that conversation is a blur of medical speak, unyielding tears and an anxiety attack of impressive proportions. My metronome began to falter slightly, and I became numb.

'But we have a plan.' There was a plan. My internal dialogue screamed many things that morning but over and over I repeated, 'Let's concentrate on this plan. Every morsel, fibre and each individual atom of my existence will focus on this plan because without a plan (regardless of what that plan is), without a plan we have nothing. Right now, be grateful for this plan.'

On a continuous loop, I stubbornly focused completely on versions of these sentences (in time to the beat of the now wavering pendulum), to the extent that I left the consultant's suite over two hours later with no understanding of the finer details of the explained plan but comforted by the fact that one existed. I was immediately propelled into an intense world which I could not comprehend, and I did not want to normalise. I fell into a massive void which was devastatingly confronting and thrust me into a monstrous vacuum, a bizarre existence. I became disenfranchised in my own body. The external world became bland and plummeted into insignificance, my micro requirements surpassed all and immediately held more value. The metronome continued to express itself vociferously, fortissimo. Brutally overwhelmed, I understood that the medical plan was to be executed with considerable haste and I had no other option to ensure success.

Although I live in Australia, my story began in Ireland. As a child I was taught that your attitude dictated your success, that positivity breeds positivity, and that you create opportunities by setting firm intentions and making them your own. I was encouraged to learn confidence, to question that which I didn't understand and to respect those who had my best interests at heart. And so, with this diagnosis, I was forced to rapidly put all my trust in the superior knowledge and understanding of the medical folk, strangers who had an intense impact on my sense of safety. Over an incredibly short space of time, I attended appointment after appointment, discussing the next necessary step in 'the plan' (with considerably more clarity and perspective than initially experienced). The metronome continued ticking, slightly off kilter, but I allowed it to become a dull background score. I asked my lists of questions, debated the options with the surgeons and my husband Simon, and followed the medical plan we agreed upon to the letter.

But it was during the days following my diagnosis (still in a mental fog with a fractured attention span), that I individually altered and controlled the trajectory of my recovery, and indeed, life. I forced myself to engage relentless optimism, to manifest only positivity (not traditionally an easy task in these circumstances), to regulate my thinking, and most significantly, my intentions. There was no epiphany, no moment of immense earth-shattering realisation, instead there were considerably more internal negotiations than devout confidence in my own mental ability to succeed. Regular demons haunted my processes, but overall, the dominant thought patterns granted me permission to cry when tears presented themselves, to yell when a cathartic release was needed, and to be kind to myself, always.

Throughout the successive weeks I consciously allowed my logical brain to take control. Ever the pragmatist, I chose to focus on the surgeon's guidance, on whatever the next medical requirement/appointment was, prepared for that whilst obsessing over the practical day-to-day needs of my children. I retreated from the world – dealing with other people's problems was not in my best interest, not at that point. I needed to maintain focus on myself, my family, my upcoming surgery, and subsequent therapy. We told only those who needed to know and asked for help from a close few. I'm wildly private and fiercely independent (often refusing to tell my right hand what's happening in my left). In times of crisis, I don't seek the approval of, or dialogue with people not directly involved. I don't need other people's opinions, fears, or influence, and those who do impose upon me – I simply set free. I reject the conjecture of well-meaning bystanders – it has hurt me in the past. Instead, I lean on and respect the views of a select number of predetermined advisers – I am firm in my belief that too many voices add a complex fog to what is often an already clouded situation.

Self-protection was an unequivocal essential. I regularly become frustrated when people offer me their 'sympathies' or 'condolences' during episodes of suffering. In my mind, their pity, grief and notions of despair served me no purpose and only proved to alleviate their personal pain. In such exchanges I feel eroded and drained, I am reminded of my suffering in a distressing way which promotes self-pity. I understand that the majority offering sympathy or stating they are 'so deeply sorry to hear of' my hardship' meant me no intentional harm but, as I dissected their words, expressions and body language, I felt like an irrelevant plot character they used to dredge up their distressing memories in an effort to feel connected and relevant. I refused to allow the crippling traits of self-pity erode or become my self-identity. Misery loves company and allows negativity to breed. This is something I could ill afford to permit to infiltrate my conscious. I needed to be mentally strong and to focus on my recovery. I chose to surround myself with those who imparted strength and encouragement, people whose solid intention was to listen first, before offering their wisdom.

I never experienced anger or felt a victim to my situation – I didn't have the energy to be despondent. Instead, I cocooned myself in a world of definite alacrity. My objective was simple: focus on being present for my family, envelope myself in care, love and optimism and nourish everything that engaged positive mental health. I acknowledged (with the initial miss-ticking of my metronome) that there were limitations to what I was capable of controlling. I was at the mercy of the Hippocratic oath; vulnerable and exposed to the superior wisdom of unfamiliar people who had spent considerably more time in academia than I had. I made a conscious decision to redirect my field of focus, to disconnect from the irrelevant, and I threw an obscene level of perspective on issues which previously would have sent my metronome into a cataclysmic spin. Emerging decisions were benchmarked against my diagnosis and I approached each individually with a new desire to change. No longer was the 'what can I control?' question paramount in my thinking; this was superseded with 'is anyone going to die if I make the wrong decision?'

The above post on social media in April 2017 was a huge, considered effort (as is penning this story). My clear and structured intention was to desperately urge the people in my life to care for themselves and as stated, to go for medical screening. I have taken upon myself a self-appointed civic duty to re-share the above post annually on the anniversary of my diagnosis. The responses received over the last four years (both publicly and privately) have been diverse, hugely unexpected, and humbling. Many of those who connected with me afterwards expressed how they were compelled to act on my suggestion and thankfully their results were clear. Some used my story to encourage others to attend to their medical needs (not necessarily within the same medical sphere as my diagnosis). Most approached my post on face value, dealing with a physical medical situation and hearing the conversation as it was spoken but some read the subtitles and addressed the mental health aspect which regularly succeed a traumatic experience of this nature.

October 2018 Social Media post:

> 'The strongest people are not those who show strength in front of us but those who win battles we know nothing about.' (Jonathan Harnisch).
>
> Two years since my diagnosis and I am winning this battle.
>
> To my beautiful darling, you have strength and you will beat this f*cker.

To my dear friends and family - now is the time, go and get checked. Xx.

This coming October will be my fifth year to offer this reminder. To date, two friends have confidentially, separately and with a guarded level of concern, contacted me to say that they found comfort in my strength and success. Both (on separate sides of the globe and from decades apart in my life) had been diagnosed with breast cancer and both felt that the timing of my post poignant (one shared with me mid-2018 and I refer to above as 'my beautiful darling'). Both friends were at incredibly vulnerable stages in their journey when sharing their story with me, but both felt compelled to connect as they took considerable meaningful solace in my medical accomplishment.

During the initial process of coping with this new label imposed upon me, digesting the finer details of this new unwelcome direction, and ensuring its impact on my children's lives was kept to a minimum, I met a wonderfully experienced medical lady who imparted the most impactful statement upon me. Her words resonated at a subconscious level and without realising, the power of her counsel held my vulnerable self vertical in an almost prophetic way. With the paraphrased statement: 'The next twelve months of your life will be difficult but with the right mental approach you will succeed. Do not allow yourself to dwell on the negative,' she imparted a marvellous strength, but paralleled that with an uncomfortable intensity.

For 'the next twelve months' I stood tall, faced the invisible torture head-on, learned to adapt and never once succumbed to any notions of not thriving. I stayed mentally strong with a stubborn intent of steel – I would walk my son (fourteen months old at the time of diagnosis) to school on his first day of kindy. My subconscious interpreted her words as instruction to comply with and to exercise every fight response available.

On the counter side, her sentence also unwittingly served me permission to collapse into a heap once the initial year passed and with spectacular abandonment my resilience and determination vanished in month thirteen. The walls collapsed and for a second time I was buried in my own catastrophic panic. My metronome (which had laid dormant for months because of my conscious decision to re-evaluate my perspective), came out to play with considerable force. But this time its effects – the dynamic which gave it power in the past – failed me. The weight of my experience dawned abruptly. Enveloped in a bleak, alien mental state of all-consuming darkness, an abyss, I disappeared.

The harsh and often neglected reality is that the pain and suffering brought on by a physical medical diagnosis does not necessarily abate itself once the physical concern is alleviated. The mental health repercussions often continue to haunt the individual in a deep, debilitating, revolting reality which exists independently for a considerable time into the future. My mental health issues were confronting, a stark reminder that, while I had been divorced and relieved of my physical complaint, I was burdened by its effects long after I closed the door on my final medical appointment.

October 2020 Social Media post:

Four years ago today I was diagnosed with breast cancer.
The first doctor I asked for help in 2016 told me it was 'probably nothing' and not to stress about it. The second opinion I sought suggested 'it would be worth investigating' ... The first consultant found 'an anomaly' which 'certainly warranted further testing' ... The second consultant advised if I wanted to see my youngest child start kindy (junior infants), surgery was my best option.

Rachel Francis

My son started kindy last February! The goodbye cuddle on his first morning meant more to me than any other parent in that classroom could understand.
Go and have whatever cancer screening is relevant for you - and always trust your gut!

Today my walls are almost rebuilt, and my metronome remains still. My experience does not define me, but it is an integral part of who I am today. It has given me a tremendous level of awareness for things that I'm willing to spend my time or energy on. Situations, people, events which once would have sent me into a spin of anxiety and distress no longer take the same control. I evaluate my world with less tolerance for minor irritations and I chose to breathe positivity with grace and dignity. Breast cancer provided me with many unwanted demons, some still loiter and probably always will. But for the most part I'm free of them. It has also given me a stalwart perspective.

Today, I live in a calmer world. My cancer story has had a lasting, powerful, and irreversible effect on me. I am reminded of it daily primarily through physical scarring, but I chose not to dwell on its damaging effects. I was unbelievably crushed on the inside; I felt my body had failed me, but I was resolute in my belief that my capacity for positivity and optimism would overcome. With an unyielding respect for the medical profession, and confidence in the medical science available, I focused my energy on walking my son to school on his first day – because this is what my consultant stated in my diagnosis appointment. I visualised my intention and was determined that nothing would take that from me.

The date 7 October represents so much in my world. It is a day we choose to celebrate as a family – there is always cake and often champagne. It is undeniable that this is the date that I received possibly the most catastrophic news of my life to date. But I refuse to obsess on the negative. Instead, I acknowledge this date as 'the day my universe operated in perfect concert' – the day my internal narrative altered its course forever, the day which forced me to reconnect with my true self and in doing so to discover my own strength, my courage and indomitable spirit. On this date, I was presented with a diagnosis that saved my life. It is because of the news that I received on that Friday morning in 2016 that I was afforded the opportunity to make decisions which ultimately led to my learning a new tempo, a new beat for my life.

Rachel Francis is an Irish Australian who was reared in Dublin in the '90s on a diet of Yeats, Heaney, Marion Keyes and Roddy Doyle, with a healthy mix of the traditional classics.

Although she continues her eclectic reading genres into adulthood, her focus and passion have guided her towards writing primarily for children with this being her first penned venture into the world of non-fiction.

Love & Loss on the Way to Mammyville

by Joanne Henry

Growing up in my time, no-one ever had that conversation that explained having a baby may be complicated and heartbreaking, or that it would take all the courage you had to keep going in the pursuit of becoming 'Mum' – or 'Mammy' if you're Irish, like me.

Yes, I learned about how a baby was made and about the labour part, I was taught that I should wait until I met someone I loved, and with whom I was happy and secure. We were also conditioned by our culture and religion to wait till we were married before starting a family.

Oh, how I wish that I were taught about the minefields I would have to wade through in the quest to reach the chosen place of 'Mammyville'! Maybe, during sex education at school we might have been introduced to the reality of pregnancy and making a baby. The highs and lows that this path can bring! Not discussing loss, miscarriage, ectopic pregnancy, and the heartbreak that is stillbirth before I was in the midst of it all, meant I was completely unprepared. If IVF and surrogacy were provided to young minds, we may have made different choices, or indeed have chosen not to have children; that too would be okay.

I believe sharing our stories is the way to help heal and to breach the gap that exists. Educating our young women and men on how to deal with these minefields at school would have better prepared us to find support and advice in these areas. Yes, there is more help and awareness out there now than there was for our parents' generation, though much more needs to be done,

Mammyville is a place where we all belong, as we have all come from one of our beloved mammies. At some time in the story of our lives, the ticking of the biological clock begins, wrapping tightly around us. In a fairytale ending, the birth happens without a hitch and we live happily ever after with our bundle of joy. Alas, real life comes a-knocking, and it might not be so simple. I hope sharing my story will bring comfort and ignite hope in women who are on this scenic route as well. Humour, which I feel the Irish are especially lucky to have in abundance, becomes the superhero cape that glides us over many a minefield and shields us from other obstacles that may come our way.

Growing up, I never had a particular number of children in mind. I just assumed, like I am sure most of us did, that we would grow up, find a partner, marry and eventually have a few kids. Sure, that is how the stories we were told go, right?

Oh, how wrong my vision on this turned out! My thirties were a haze of highs and lows while I trod this path. It is here we enter the chapter that highlights the high of that first positive test and then the sadness of early miscarriage. Do not worry, the doctors said, this is perfectly normal, your body just getting ready, so you pick yourself up and keep hope alive. The next journey is full of complications, and the threatening miscarriage – a word we once did not know existed – was taking over our lives. We then hit the depths of despair when our precious baby

Jacob arrived prematurely and did not survive. We were plunged into a dark, dark place and the innocence of pregnancy was buried, along with our precious baby. To say hello and goodbye to your firstborn in the same breath, for labour to end in silence, to bury your firstborn, is incomprehensible. It impacts not only your life, but a ripple effect goes out to your entire family.

No-one teaches you about this possible chapter in life. Why? I guess it is just such an awful thing that the world does not want to acknowledge, and I guess even today it is still a taboo subject. Do I think this is the wrong way? Hell yeah! Did this experience change us? No doubt. We were left heartbroken, and the ache that began on that day for our son will remain forever – as time goes on, it is just not as loud.

The next chapter we embarked on involved dealing with our grief, which involved feeling bereft and wondering, 'Am I a mammy?' 'How can I be a mammy when my baby is no longer with me?' 'Will I ever have a baby?' 'Is it fair on my hubby?' The fight for sanity was a hard one. It was hard on our relationship, it was a roller-coaster, but we fought hard – even when we did not want to. We read books, we attended support groups – well, one session, and it was all that we needed to ignite hope. In one group a man said something that made us laugh in the car afterwards: that this experience can either bring you together or blow your relationship out of the water. After tears flowed in the meeting, we sat in the car and my other half turned and repeated the statement back in a serious tone. We then both looked at each other and burst into laughter, great big belly laughs, tears rolling down our cheeks. In between gulps we pledged to swim this damn river of grief and not let us be blown out of the water. That night got us through the crazy journey of another pregnancy, another miscarriage, another scary pregnancy and more bed rest, until finally we had weathered the crazy storm. Our rainbow was finally here in the form of Hannah (Hannah banana to family). Looking down at that mop of McGarvey hair and the chubby face, we agreed that all the sorrow and heartbreak was worth it.

We moved into a stage of contentment after this, and it was not until our precious daughter's teacher congratulated us on my pregnancy – which wasn't true – that we realised our daughter, having heard her school friends sharing news of siblings being born, had decided she wanted one too. Now I was blessed to have a stepson when I married my husband, but there was a big age gap and Hannah only saw him on the days he spent with his dad. After that awkward parents' meeting, when the poor teacher was so embarrassed, and after we all laughed about how children say the funniest things, it got me thinking. I wondered if we should embark on this scary pregnancy route again, to give Hannah a sibling to grow up with.

We decided to try, and we would stop when I turned forty if nothing had happened. Our dreams came true and I fell pregnant at thirty-nine. It seemed like it was all falling into place, but alas another heartbreak occurred: an ectopic pregnancy was confirmed, another taboo subject we were not prepared for.

My first thought was sadness, seeing a heartbeat on the screen and being told it is in the wrong place and could not continue. Secondly, I felt angry. Why would God let this happen, let me get pregnant when I was just coming to the point of accepting it may not happen again. Giving us hope and then taking it back seemed so cruel and unfair. We had so much to give, and it seemed that people who did not want kids, some who did not deserve them, could fall pregnant so easily. Lastly, I had to get my head around the fact that this pregnancy must end, surgically, as it could be fatal for me. Effectively, I had to terminate my baby before it could harm me. Hard to process for sure, my head knew it was the right thing to do, but my heart ached.

I ended up losing a fallopian tube and was incredibly lucky to survive due to complications with the surgery. It ended with a blood transfusion and a long recovery period, and we had to come to the sad conclusion that our baby chapter was over, a decision that was so hard when I knew I could still get pregnant, but the risks were too high. I had a beautiful daughter who needed me here, so getting my heart and mind around that decision took a while. Years later, something triggered negative thoughts about pregnancy. I was not even aware myself of the trauma that ten years of fertility issues had caused. Thankfully, I sought help, and now I am at peace with myself and the negative thinking is under control. I know a lot of people still suffer in silence out of shame, not wanting to make a fuss, and end up going through life untreated.

As a consequence of my journey, I am now so passionate about maternal health. It gives me hope when I see changes in the aftercare that is out there for women and couples who have dealt with the trauma of loss in pregnancy – although there is still a lot more to be done.

Women deserve to be supported, loss needs to be treated like the trauma it is and recovery must be offered. Anniversaries will always be hard, but with support, couples will learn that it is okay and normal to feel low at these times. In time it does get easier, we never forget but we will smile again.

Eleven years on, on the run-up to Jacob's anniversary, I still remember every detail of that time: the names of the nurses, the doctors, the kind words and the not so kind words. At the moment our world stood still, when they said, 'I'm sorry, you're going into labour and your baby will die.' I did not recognise the scream that was released from my body as my own, it sounded so animalistic and broken. It always seems to run like a video tape through my mind at this time of year. Of course, while I was feeling bereft that I did not have my baby, friends and family members were pregnant and going on to have their own, healthy babies. Fortunately, I was able to separate my feelings and be happy for them.

Education is essential to break the silence and to help families heal when they are going through this loss. We love to be able to speak of our babies and should never be uncomfortable. Remembering helps the healing process, tiny footprints are forever etched on our hearts. Not a day goes by that I do not think of my losses or of my baby Jacob. He is always my first and last thought. This does not mean that I talk about him every day, but if I do, or if I meet someone who has lost a child, I never shy away from the topic. This means I want to talk and feel comfortable to share our story with you.

On reflection, eleven years later I can see that it was important to begin fighting from those early days, even though I was so sad and exhausted, mentally and physically. I had spent two weeks in hospital fighting to keep my son from being born. I had the signs of having had a baby but no baby in my arms. Something else I was not prepared for, my milk came in. No-one told me to prepare for this. I could feel my body preparing to nurture the baby I had given birth to, yet the baby was no longer here. Oh, I had wished that I had been told to prepare for this. Although as I said, eleven years ago things were different.

My fight started with words – literally – on a page. My husband and friends, who all work in this field, encouraged me to keep a 'mood diary'. I was not eager, and I think I used a few choice words, believing they thought I had lost the plot and was being treated as a patient. You see, I am a mental health nurse by day, and these were the tools I taught my patients when they hit a minefield with their mental health.

On reflection, I was a patient who needed help, but at that time I was not seen as one. The medical team had helped me in a physical sense, to deliver my baby, attend my wounds, and discharge me as medically fit, handing me kind words and a leaflet. I know now that I really should have been given more aftercare for my mental and emotional wellbeing. This was an area back then that was not given the credibility it deserved, nor the financial input to deliver that service. This is still an area that needs to be improved, but I can see things are changing for the better, albeit slowly.

Looking back, I was lucky in having the support and understanding of my partner, family, and friends. With encouragement, I started that mood diary and slowly realised it was helping me. I had a visual aid to track improvements in my mood. I worked out my pain and anger in that little book, especially in those early months when I was just so sad. I didn't leave the house for six weeks, and when I finally did, I shopped outside my town. We left our trolley in a supermarket aisle on one occasion as seeing too many newborn babies caused my heart to explode in pain.

Each night I let out all these emotions onto the pages of my diary. I wrote a note to myself at the beginning of the book telling myself to write in it each night, even if I did not want to, as I knew it would help. I still have that diary in a box, along with my son Jacob's blanket, the pictures that were taken of him – they are so precious to me now. I named him Jacob as soon as I knew I was pregnant with him. I had awful morning sickness, well, actually all-day sickness – another taboo they never tell you about. It was one night in the wee hours that I was sitting eating a dry cream cracker to help with the nausea that I noticed 'Jacobs' on the packet and thought, *Oh, that is a nice boy's name!* I never really told anyone that, as I found that after you lose a child sometimes people feel uncomfortable when you talk about them. I know that this must change also.

It took time for me to have the courage to talk to new people who did not know my story about my son. I often don't mention it, even now, until I know people a bit, then I feel guilty. If this taboo were broken, people like me would feel less awkward about mentioning their children who are no longer here.

I am one of the lucky ones, yes, I had a scenic route to Mammyville as I got my 'rainbow baby' - a term used to describe the baby you have after experiencing the storm of loss through miscarriage or stillbirth. My pregnancy with my rainbow child Hannah was fraught with fear and anxiety, with bed rest to ensure she stayed safe and made no early appearance, like Jacob had. I do not think anyone realises that, after a mother has gone through the trauma of loss, pregnancy is always scary, right up until you get that baby safe in your arms. You are afraid to believe, this time, that all will be well. I suppose on reflection it is you trying to protect your heart by not letting yourself get excited until you know all is well. I am glad to see that these fears and anxieties are now acknowledged, and mothers will have support through future pregnancies.

Having gone through the scenic route of pregnancy, my passion for maternal health has been ignited. I love to hear stories of women and their partners who have gone to great lengths to get their baby: IVF, surrogacy and adoption, many finally succeeding after multiple losses. Some have decided that enough was enough and have come to terms that they will close the door on that chapter of their life. I am sure that is a hard decision to make and should be supported.

What I have learned from reading and hearing stories about other people's journeys is that women are resilient, brave, courageous and unstoppable at times, despite the pain, heartache and stress we face in our quest to become a mammy. We are unsung warriors, we rise up in spite of obstacles, and become stronger, empathetic and amazing role models to future generations. So, if you are reading this and have gone through trauma relating to fertility and are still struggling seek help, do it, because you are worth it. Rise like a phoenix and help us help our fellow women. Using the power of words, let's share how we have overcome adversity and help others heal. Words have such power, they help ignite hope, comfort and, most importantly, educate. I am proud to be a woman and not afraid to roar. Are you?

Joanne Henry is a forty-four-year-old nurse by day and writer by night. She is author of *Memoirs of a Mad Mammy* (2020).
She is mammy to the lovely Hannah and step-mammy to Dylon, and, of course, fur-mammy to the gorgeous Jessie. She is also wife to long-suffering husband, making up the dysfunction that is the Henry family.
Joanne loves to write and believes that sharing stories helps others to heal.

Obstacles are things that frighten you when you take your eyes off the road.

— Kez Wickham St George

Colour Matching
by Julia Kaylock

When I was eight years old, Margaret informed me that everybody's name has a colour. Margaret and I would often spend some of the holidays together as we were the last two cousins in a long line, separated from the rest by a good ten years. Margaret was always emphatic – and bossy, with me anyway – I was obviously easy prey. So, one day when we sat down on our aunties' back porch, we discussed the colours of our relatives' names. Well, Margaret discussed, and I ended up agreeing. It was easier that way; I listened as she wrote down 'Marjorie yellow' (when it was clearly red) and 'Olive brown' (did she not know that olive was a green colour?), but with no input into the game my imagination quelled more quickly than it had been sparked.

I honestly don't remember my colour, but I am pretty sure it would not have been purple, which, if you asked me now, would be the colour I would connect with my name, with me. Purple – a commanding colour, dark and brooding while standing out, especially in the company of other colours. I don't align with the concept of 'royal purple', or Christian religion purple (which are, in fact, modern attachments), and it was only as an adult that I found out that purple symbolises magic, mystery, spirituality, dignity, creativity – and the subconscious. Yes, if my eight-year-old self was wiser and more confident, she would have been emphatic that her name meant purple.

I wasn't always called Julia. The name I was given at the time of my adoption was much more, well, 'frilly', so I guess it wasn't all my cousin's fault. The way my mother clothed me didn't help; she was a keen seamstress, and I was her not-so-willing model. Mum loved to embellish, anything she made for me had lots of lace, ribbons and buttons. Add brilliant white socks and patent-leather shoes, and that was me, sent out into the world with a warning not to get dirty, which did not allow much room for childhood fun. This is how I came to be sitting on the porch outside my aunties' house (there were two of them, one married, one single) with my cousin, who was dressed in overalls and gumboots, the perfect gear for collecting chook eggs. The memory of this day is so strong, I can still feel those eggs on my lap, warm, smooth, and somehow, comforting. The bantam eggs were so cute, they had speckles. We were going to have them for lunch. No, it was not her fault that Margaret probably identified me and my name with some other, bland shade – pastel pink? Or maybe, baby blue.

Even in my quiet, submissive state, on that day I was purple, seething inside like a volcano ready to erupt, but I didn't know that then. I had locked myself away, because I was afraid of me – of the real me, who was clearly not someone acceptable to society, because whenever she peeped out behind defiant eyes, or shouted through clenched teeth, she was chastised, shut down, ignored. So I was careful to be the girl I was supposed to be that day, sitting on my aunties' porch, afraid to yell at my cousin, afraid to dirty my clothes, afraid of – well, everything I suppose; but the question should never have been 'what' I was afraid of, but 'why' was I afraid. That question was never asked, and without the necessary answer to this very important, unasked question, I lived for many years in a state of constant confusion.

At the age of eight, I didn't know I was adopted. I just knew that I didn't fit; I was in the wrong place with the wrong people. I lived in a house with 'Mummy and Daddy', and my big brother who was twelve years older than me. I was often reminded that I was on probation, threats to evict me were common, and without really understanding why, I knew I was only there by their good grace. I needed to play the good girl, it was a survival issue, so except for a few highlights, life was monotone. I was often starved for company, so became quite good at storytelling as a way of relieving the boredom. I kept my stories to myself, as they were made up and I was only allowed to tell the truth. Emotions didn't live in our house either, especially ones that involved crying our shouting.

Of stoic Christian stock, my family never shared their deepest darkest secrets, I therefore learned nothing of the pain of miscarriage, of my mother wanting a big family but who, even after several attempts to have another baby, found it impossible to carry one to full term. It was because of what we know now as the Rhesus factor, the antibodies in Mum's blood attacked the foetuses and killed them off. Had I known this much earlier in my life, I know I would have been understanding.

I have always been a compassionate soul, which my family thought was a defect, so they kept everything that was unpleasant from me. For example, I was never told about my lovely cat being killed on the road, she simply 'disappeared'. I did not learn of my Aunty Olive's protracted battle with cancer, it was kept a secret until my mother came home one day, dressed to the nines, and announced that her sister had died. I was not allowed to attend funerals or to grieve anyone's death. I was just told that we wouldn't be visiting them any longer.

It is not surprising, then, that I had no idea about my adoptive mother's struggles, nor did I know anything about another woman, somewhere far away, who had given birth to me and then left me at the hospital. Did she leave me? Was it free will, or was she forced to sign me over? I will never know, because that lady died when I was just sixteen.

That time in my life sticks in my memory, because I was being constantly watched, more than I had ever felt previously. I was no longer allowed to do things I had always done, like Saturday trips to the beach with friends, playing sports and going to parties. I knew this was because I was what my parents thought of as 'troubled', a problem who needed watching in case she – in case she what? I heard them talking at night in the kitchen, while I was supposed to be asleep.

They were talking about me, but I had no concept of me, or why I was troubled. I remember making a scene because my mother didn't want me to have a black dress, but I wanted one so badly that she finally bought me one. I had worn her down, she said to one of her sisters, making me wonder who was troubled, me, or her, and not for the first time.

Mum was unwell throughout many of my teenage years, she became very anaemic and there was talk of a heart condition, her thin frame had become more bird-like and the doctors could not work out what was wrong with her. Again, I wasn't told much, but I took on most of the chores: washing the clothes in the twin-tub washer, hanging them on the line, bringing them in and then ironing everything and putting it all away. I cooked the meals, and then washed the dishes while my father and brother sat in front of the TV. I don't remember being told to do those things, but I knew it was expected, and I somehow felt Mum being sick was my fault, so I kept myself busy and avoided her even more.

I always felt I needed to earn my place in the household. The feeling of temporariness is something that was with me throughout my childhood. With my mother's words about sending me away 'to the reformatory' still ringing in my ears, as a teenager I started looking for other places to go in case that threat was actually ever carried out. I scoped friends' houses for possibilities, but as I was moving into the final two years of school I made the decision to go to a university that took boarders. I worked out which course I would do and attended open days. I knew I would need a part-time job to pay for the room so started doing casual work wherever I could, in preparation. By the end of year 11 I was all set to branch out on my own and was counting down the months till the HSC exams.

My plans unravelled a few months later, when, halfway through year 12 I became ill. Very ill. Nobody, not even the doctors, could work out what was wrong, but I was laid up for a couple of months and it was a slow recovery back to full health, so I had to repeat year 12 the following year. I later learned that my illness was the start of a lifetime in which everything I did, any plans I made, would be overshadowed by chronic fatigue syndrome (now called ME), that would lead to many annoying health issues, laying me low for protracted periods of time.

Back to year 12! I still had the same plan, but I had started seeing a young man who went to my church, he was troubled for different reasons and wanted to leave home even more urgently than I did. We thought we would move together to Adelaide where things were cheaper, but as luck would have it, he was offered a job with his company in Melbourne. We were engaged shortly after I completed my HSC and, two months later, he moved to Melbourne. Eight months later I followed; thoughts of university were put on hold, for now.

On arrival in Melbourne I decided to shorten my name. Nobody would ever slip up and call me by my real name if they had no idea what it was. Free from parental restraint, I started to work out my true colours, to find out who I really was. I was intent on trying out as many different shades and hues as possible – and as it was the '70s, there was lots of colour to be had. I am not just talking about actual colours, I was intent on lapping up all the things life had to offer – some were definitely not things my strict churchgoing family would have approved of: drinking alcohol, smoking cigarettes, dancing, using swear words and sharing the occasional joint. David and I also got involved in rally driving and horse riding, two activities that my mother thought would surely lead to injury or death. From a distance, I enjoyed filling her in on some of the things I got up to – not all of them, I still cared enough to not want her to die from worry.

As my twenties progressed, I began to become suspicious about my roots. Things I had overlooked in my younger, fearful years, started to become signs: a homework assignment that involved collecting details of my family members' blood types, a request for my birth certificate when I wanted to get my learner's permit, whispers from people in the church when they thought I was out of range. At twenty-seven, I became a real-life detective into my own life and discovered the truth.

> *Purple, the colour of a plump aubergine*
> *Smash it and watch its insides scream*
> *That's the rage on the page of my history*
> *The curtain's been lifted, now I can see.*
> *Don't you dare tell me, it was for my own good,*
> *Don't even try to say you're misunderstood,*
> *See my face, stained with tears,*
> *Hear my voice ringing loudly in your ears?*
> *I am purple and proud,*
> *I'm ferocious and loud,*
> *There's a ship, it's in motion,*

It's as deep as the ocean
From lies I am free,
Watch the roll of the sea;
I've found a new rhythm,
Catch the light from the prism
These are fractals, aren't they pretty, see?
Watch them dance – these are The Colours of Me.

My 'discovery' that I was adopted led to a great deal of pain and grief. Like any form of grief, it is impossible to describe the nature or depth of the emotions it created. It came in waves, and attached itself to different feelings and responses at different times. I did not learn for a while that the mother who gave birth to me had died while I was still a teenager, meaning I would never get to meet her. With that knowledge, a whole new variety of grief enveloped me. It is, I have found, impossible for those brought up within their 'biological' families to understand the extent to which complex PTSD infiltrates the lives of adoptees who were forcibly removed from their mothers, so I won't even try. I do know, though, from personal experience, that it is entirely possible to operate one's life whilst in the grip of grief – we humans are experts at this. What I have found though, is that that even after I got over my fearful teens and wasteful twenties, even after my life became one of purpose, this thing called grief remained, and has sat alongside me all the way, in one guise or another.

Those who have known me for any length of time will say I am a happy, confident and resourceful person. I am often told that I am brave, that I have achieved a great deal. I have to say, I have lived a busy and full life.

Compared to many, my life has been easy. I have never been homeless, I have been well-fed and never wanted, materially at least, for anything. I have studied to Masters level and amassed a swag of credentials in the counselling and coaching fields, I have travelled extensively, I have a wonderful and resilient husband, beautiful children and grandchildren. I live in one of the best places in the world. I have also been a writer and editor for three decades. I certainly have lived a rainbow-coloured life.

A rainbow is gorgeous, but what is behind the rainbow? For the sake of consistency, let's call it purple - the still purple waters of the deep. Purple grief. Purple sits somewhere deep in my soul, coming out obliquely in the words I say and write, in the way I respond to events and in the face of injustice. So, as I write yet another version of my story, I wonder at the tenacity of grief. I have come to think of it as a constant companion – I won't call it a friend – who spices up my life, so whenever I get complacent, or, heaven help me, feel happy, it is there to reveal something new to me.

Shall I illustrate? The year that started in September 2012 was a purple year, one that required all of the tenacity, resourcefulness, patience and adaptability I had developed over a lifetime. It was a year when I worked out what I truly was capable of achieving, I found my strengths, my weaknesses, and along the way, a missing piece of my soul. It was a year of threats to everything I held dear, my purpose, my *raison d'etre*. It de-centred me and challenged everything I had learned about life.

The story starts at the end of a busy era in which I had achieved a great deal, professionally and personally. I was ready to relax for a while, to take a breath or two after being made redundant. I was not in great mental or physical health, having put in all kinds of hours through a period of significant change at the university where I was working. I am not one to be idle for long, though, and despite my exhaustion, during my final weeks of work I was excited to be launching a company with a colleague, developing programs specifically for students with disabilities.

As we launched our new venture, I received news that my father, who lived interstate, was experiencing his end of days. He finally passed on, peacefully, in early December of that year, just over two months after my last day of work at the uni, not long after we spoke for the last time. He died with no regrets and still no answers to my questions about my adoption – I grieved his death, we had shared many wonderful times together, but with his passing another door to my truth closed forever.

After Dad and Mum were united once more – I hope in heaven for that was their fervent desire – I arrived home utterly exhausted. I was in the midst of reassembling when it became obvious that the cracks in my thirty-eight-year marriage had built to the point of being a danger to my wellbeing. David had found himself increasingly in the grip of alcoholism and the strain on our relationship was becoming unbearable. In the days following I summoned the courage to issue an eviction order. He left that day, contrite, confused and shocked, as I demanded he hand me the keys to our city unit and to never return.

The eviction order was surprisingly easy, as it turned out, but unwinding the tangled mess of four decades proved to be a lot more complicated. Our eldest daughter was getting married in two months, she was determined he would not attend, unless he proved that he had truly given up the drink this time. With an alacrity that I had not previously witnessed, he pleaded his way into a rehab program – the intake nurse saw that he was genuine and bumped him to the head of the queue. For Christmas that year my youngest daughter got me a kitten – I can honestly say this little man saved my mental health during this period, and on several other occasions since, for one reason and another.

After our daughter's wedding (which was attended, in fact, by all the family) I found myself living alone for the first time in my life. Fortunately, I soon had news that a grandbaby was on the way and I was busy with the new business, including coordinating a series of seminars and workshops around Australia, to be led by a disability expert from the UK. I was also enmeshed in a difficult situation regarding my father's estate, involving several trips to Sydney, now realising that I had been sidelined by my brother and his wife, I was essentially a family outcast. Despite his final words: 'We must see more of each other now; it is just the two of us,' said with a solemn face as I left Sydney for the last time, I have not had one phone call, text or email from him in almost eight years.

Back in Melbourne, the apartment was even lonelier, our youngest daughter had gone overseas to work, so it was just me and the kitten, who, whether he liked it or not, became my confidante and wise counsellor. He was a very agreeable companion who listened attentively and never argued. Except for work, I was avoiding the company of others, even though I felt exceedingly lonely, especially at night.

What kept me buoyed was making the final arrangements for my 'trip of a lifetime', which I had been planning as a gift to myself since before I left the university, using some of my redundancy payment. The scheduled departure date was 29 August 2013, I would be travelling for six weeks, starting in Budapest, Hungary and travelling through Austria, Croatia, the Balkans and finally, spending two weeks touring around Turkey. I was so excited about this trip, it felt so wonderfully exotic to be travelling to these mysterious countries. I had done all the usual countries: France, Italy, Greece etc. with David and the girls, but taking an extended trip solo felt like I was really coming of age as a traveller.

I needed this trip badly. I needed to escape the Melbourne cold and get outside myself as well, to regroup and to reconfigure my life. I was in a purple haze and needed to find my rainbow colours again.

Unfortunately, this trip did not eventuate. Well. I did get to Budapest, but instead of strolling around ancient streets and eating delicious food, I found myself quickly on a plane again, my holiday of a lifetime becoming a nine-day stint in a Mexican hospital where our youngest daughter was fighting for her life following a serious accident. She survived, but then came the news that she might lose her right arm. Our other daughter was back at home, unable to work and needing support also due to complications with her pregnancy. David was spending all his spare time (when he was not working or in his alcohol recovery program that continued one day each week) gathering information for our return home and talking to staff about further operations and ongoing treatment for our daughter at The Alfred Hospital.

Almost one year to the day after I finished full-time work, my daughter and I were back in Australia, with much work left to do on all fronts. For the next six months I would be her carer – a role for which I was ill-equipped, but like all the challenges I had faced, I embraced it and did my best to ensure the best possible outcome for her. Seven years after almost losing her life, our youngest qualified as a Registered Nurse – a career she embraced out of gratitude to the medical system and the wonderful people who saved her. Our eldest is a mother to three lovely children, and my marriage of now forty-six years, has survived and has thrived!

A fairytale ending? Not quite. The purple phase was far from over, it was not done with me yet, not by a long shot. Somehow, though, purple saved me, and remade me into the woman I am today: a survivor.

Julia Kaylock is a qualified counsellor, adult educator, career practitioner and coach, who has operated her own consultancy for twenty-one years. Her work also involves project management, writing and editing.

Julia's first love is poetry, and in addition to being widely published in poetry journals and anthologies, she has edited and co-edited a number of combined works including *Messages from the Embers: from devastation to hope* (Black Quill Press, 2020), an anthology of poetry in response to the 2019-2020 Australian bushfire, and *Poetry for the Plant: an anthology of imagined futures* is due for publication in October 2021.

www.litoriapress.com

Peeling Back the Layers

by Holly Rose Holland

I scheduled a visit with a friend who lived near my parents' house. It was April; she offered me a reiki appointment at her home. I did not even know what reiki was, but thought it was some sort of exercise. For a reason unknown to me, I felt I had to go. I made sure I was welcome to bring my mom along as we would be stopping on our way to another city to shop. This was the first time I became truly aware of my chakras, and I felt an energy presence. During the reiki I was visited by someone who had died, they liked to play a lot of jokes and this continued into the afterlife: they turned the music off. They could do that?

I grew up knowing when births and deaths were about to happen. Notice of a birth or death arrived at night, in my sleep. Sometimes it would be a specific person, but usually I simply felt that a birth or death was about to happen. Most of the time, the birth or death occurred the next day. In addition, I would get a feeling of knowing whether I should or should not do something. This seemed to be a natural way to make a decision without putting much thought into it. 'Going with my gut' is how I saw it then; now I refer to it as my inner voice. I always loved gardening, as that was a family activity that I enjoyed, and it helped family members as well. There was colour sprinkled throughout the yard. We grew fruit, vegetables and flowers that attracted hummingbirds. In the past year, I have recognised the importance of grounding. This is a central factor in intuition.

Registering for a transformational healing in May, I did not know what it was or why I went, but my intuition again told me to go. I became extremely relaxed while I was there and received a lot of energy during the healing. At the healing you could ask for help with something, or to be given an answer that would help guide you in your life. You could ask for help with knee pain, for example. My interest in this type of healing peaked. I was uncertain why I liked it, but I attended once a month. Often, people attending the healings have many of the same things that need to be worked on. This is not a plan; it just happens that way. If there is something that could be of benefit to you, you will also receive it, being part of the group. The organisers were planning to host a retreat to Greece in the fall. I paid little attention since I had booked a writer's retreat in Northern Ireland for the same month.

Prior to the reiki and transformational healing, I started writing. I reserved a room at a beautiful castle in Northern Ireland where I would meet many of the women I had been networking with virtually. This was the opportunity of a lifetime. I knew I had always wanted to write a book, and it seemed like the perfect time. I wanted to help people who were stuck because of many kinds of loss, such as death, lifestyle, relationship and employment.

In August, I booked my flights to and from Ireland. Limited options for flights were available. I planned to add ten days to my trip but could not make the flights work past seven days. The day after I booked, the transformational healing notice for the trip to Greece arrived. The retreat was starting the day I was leaving Ireland. Feeling this was a sign, I rescheduled my flights and added the Greece retreat to the Ireland trip.

The retreat at the castle was a magical experience: history, comradery, nature, writing, amazing meals, and predominantly, networking. The next week was a Serenity Press writing retreat. I joined them for a couple of days, which included the high tea. It was a lovely opportunity to meet Karen McDermott's community of authors. While I was with Karen's group, I realised I was indeed a writer and a soon to be published author. We talked at length about all kinds of things, went on nature walks and had some lovely meals. Several authors gave me some amazing advice about writing and we had some heartfelt talks. I had spent years looking for a writing job. Could it be that I just had to write? I focused on writing at the castle and looked forward to continuing to write and edit my book about my grief journey.

Writing has been the greatest gift to me. It always was a gift, even as a child. I kept a blog during my husband's illness and eventual death. The first thing people said was that I should find a job in writing. I did not know becoming an author would be the answer to a lot of these questions. It is such a gift to put the words down. I never expected something as simple as writing in a journal to have such a value in keeping a person moving. When the words are on the page, sometimes the greatest benefit is when you go back and read it. Many times, while I am journaling, I am just letting the words flow from the heart to the pen. When I read it back, I am usually surprised at what I wrote on the page. The ideas keep flowing and I have been busy getting them into spoken and written form.

When I left the writing retreat, I had a book with me that was written by Bernadette O'Connor, called *Beneath the Veil,* which was very thought-provoking. We had talked at length about many aspects of writing, and I could not help but wonder if I had hinted about this part of my past. I became absorbed in this book during my flight to Greece.

The steward served a delicious meal during the second leg of the flight. The rest of my row was empty, a private space to get lost in the book. When the steward spoke to me about my dinner, I was so engrossed in the book that I screamed. I am not sure how many people I scared on the plane, but I was unaware of what was going on around me. I continued reading after I arrived at my hotel that evening, and again the next morning. This book has two distinct stages: dread and despair at the beginning, and the path to new ways of living life at the end. I halted at the transition point in the book. I tried picking it up to finish it several times while I was in Greece. I tried again to finish it during the many flights home, without success. I realised then that I needed to examine some things in my past. The dark parts in O'Connor's book closely aligned with events of my past, but while her story was personal, mine related to business. I did not know then that I was about to start a journey to unravel the complicated parts of my life.

In Greece, there were several days of transformational healings. The environment has a lot of history, we visited ruins that exuded the history of the place, and with this came intense energy. Participants shared transformational healing with others in the group. When healings are held in deeply historical places, the energy can lead to intense transformational experiences. Examples of an intensified experience could be an extreme emotion, unique or loud sounds, and different languages spoken by people that are not aware they can speak that language. These experiences are unique to each person, people will experience what is best for them at that moment in their life. A 'movie of abuse' kept playing in my mind while in Greece, and it was hard to focus. My experience included confusion, as I did not recognise this movie, and heat trying to escape my body. These were not hot flashes, but the heat was intense and felt internally. This was a very uncomfortable experience in this beautiful tropical environment that was hot enough already. I remember thinking I should have worn a wet bathing suit to keep cool.

During transformation I was honestly worried and afraid of revealing something, I was not ready to heal completely, but I was starting to open up. This type of healing has many steps and it takes time to process. I have always experienced situations as movies playing in my head. I thought they played like that for everyone. I spent most of my life thinking those were dreams. I discovered many of them were about things that had happened to me, or to someone I knew in the past. When they were not positive, I always told myself not to think about them.

When I returned home, I attended an intensive transformational healing with an expert visiting the Edmonton area, near my home in Alberta, Canada. A friend advised me to release any past events that still affected me, as far as I was comfortable with, emphasising that I could expedite healing by working on it right there and then. I brought forward information about abuse I had experienced. Most of the incidents were of mental abuse, with some having sexual suggestion. There were repetitive patterns. We talked through some events, a need to make stronger boundaries, and to make myself a higher priority. I realised that I had kept quiet about some incidents in order to keep other people's lives from changing. While I was trying to protect people's reputations, this clearly failed for me in a personal sense. The expectation was that I would keep all the incidents to myself, as if nothing had happened. Although I was really just getting started, this day was an enormous shift for me, as if I had reached the core. Now I could work my way out.

I began exploring and taking part in more intuitive modalities. The first one was Akashic records: all records of the past, present and future in the entire universe, including what has happened and how people feel about them. Once I talked through more concerns about abuse, repeating patterns and setting boundaries in the records, I found I could start reading the rest of Bernadette's book and finished it. Now my healing experiences changed to feeling extremely cold, which was the complete opposite to the heat I felt in Greece. I could finish writing my story, *Keep Moving, Creating a Life After Loss* to help people experience another way. It was a long journey getting that first book of mine down on paper and then doing the editing. It was just so raw to remember the way it used to be, when everything was new and I was not sure how to continue life and to face the challenges within my core value of honesty. The hardest part of the editing was dealing with all the emotions. I could hardly believe I could make myself cry every time, except for the very last proofread.

I continued with the meditation I started about three years prior. My meditation practice has changed a lot over the years. At one time, I only meditated at home and for about forty minutes. I used to set a timer. Then I meditated morning, night and anytime I could not get back to sleep, using a meditation app. Later I did many short meditations for five minutes at a time. Now what I do is mostly meditate during walks. The walk can be up to seventy-five minutes and it is usually two or three blocks of time, so it is not as deep a meditation as I would like it to be. I often find that meditating for as little as five minutes can be enough to help to ground me and to move me into a different mind space. On a chaotic day, even two minutes can be helpful. I can use the time in the elevator or when I take the stairs. My favourite time to do meditation is when there is no time limit. Leading a busy life, this does not happen often, but it is so amazing to just start meditating and just almost get lost in it, to see where getting deeper into my mind takes me. I think that is why I love these various types of intuition, because they will take me to deeper parts of my whole being. To write down the experience is helpful but the most benefit and understanding is through experiencing it for oneself. Thinking of it in the same way as a sound is the closest comparison I can make; describing a high-pitched sound is not as easy to imagine as having a high-pitched sound vibrating throughout your body. Some people prefer to imagine it as colour. I found meditation to be a good practice to maintain when working on things from the past, it helped to ground me and keep me calm.

Examining two separate instances was essential to my healing. With one job, I was filling in for a co-worker who was on vacation. The boss decided I would work in the front. I had never used the equipment before, which included a telex and word processor. The telex was the method used for sending tenders. As the message was sent, it was received in real time with no opportunity to correct mistakes. A paper tape punched out the message. For the second and subsequent recipients, the punched tape had to be fed through the machine again after dialling the next phone number. The paper tape jammed in the machine while it was sending to the next recipient. I found out later that if the tape ripped or jammed, information would be missing. The boss was hot-tempered and became angry when he heard about the machine jamming. He also needed some work done on a word processor. I did not even know where the power button was. There was not a lot of work done; something happened that still gives me shivers. Breathing heavily, the boss leaned over me while I sat on a chair in front of the word processor. He was very close. I froze. I do not remember what the conversation was after that, other than I remained frozen on the chair. I obviously left at some stage. I was very clear that I would not take part in whatever he was planning. It was as if the day had stopped. He never pulled that leaning over trick again, but my recollection of it is as vivid today as the day it happened – over thirty years ago.

The second incident also involved work in a front office, except that this time it was my usual place of work. On my first day, my co-workers clearly told me to always stay in the primary office, not to go to any satellite buildings with anyone, including a manager. Forgetting this, one day I phoned the manager to ask for help with something new. As there was no answer, I walked to his office. His solution was to forget about the customers, lock his office door and simply get 'cozy' with me in his office. Although people had warned me of a potential danger, his words were still shocking. I gave him my 'not a chance' look. I could not leave the job soon enough.

These two experiences occurred when I was just nineteen. When I became brave enough to speak up, another woman quickly trivialised these incidents, seeing them as minor compared to her own experience. I obviously picked the wrong woman to talk to about this, but I never spoke to her again. Years later, a student from a local university approached the business where I worked with a survey. As I completed the survey, I realised how frequently in my life abuse had occurred. Until this point, the right or ability to stop it had never occurred to me. It did not help that I realised how often abuse occurred in a place that was assumed to be safe. I hope workplace safety programs prevent these types of abuse from occurring nowadays.

Reiki is the intuitive area that I really found clarity and calm in. As someone who needed some help with pain, it has been amazing. When I had just started treatment with an intuitive energy-based chiropractor, the pandemic caused everything to stop. I was quite worried at that point because it was quite a critical time and I had barely started going for treatments and getting relief. I had taken the first level of reiki just ten days prior. I could benefit from doing reiki on myself to keep my pain manageable and to help me to remain calm – very important during a pandemic. People have their own personal experience giving and receiving reiki. I find it very relaxing to receive and will fall asleep. When giving reiki, the giver feels heat flowing from their body and the receiver will often report feeling this heat as well. It is a very calming experience for both. I find colour provides healing power.

Over time, the pain I had been experiencing subsided. Three weeks into my self-reiki, the brace I was wearing to bed at night to keep my wrist straight was no longer needed. That was over one year ago, and I have only worn the brace a few nights since. It amazed me to discover I could help myself that much. I go to the chiropractor for fine tuning treatments, while I continue to provide a lot of benefit for myself. I have a lifetime of injuries that I need to work through, and some of them are harder to adjust than others. Being able to address some physical parts myself has been invaluable.

When I first noticed the gold-coloured energy, it was rarely visible. Now that I am paying attention, it is visible every day. I find it is so brilliant on the snowy days but honestly, as long as there is light, I can see and feel the energy all around. In the dark, I feel the energy. It is puzzling how we can ignore things we feel and see around us, like movement in the air. We can dismiss things so quickly: 'That is just how it looks around my glasses,' or, 'When I just turn my head kind of quickly I see …' I feel such gratitude and excitement that my intuition is being heightened, but I realise now it has always been here. I am now actively using and experiencing my intuition.

There was still another mystery to unravel. I knew that a lot of patterns repeated many times in my life, and I didn't understand why. Months of self-reiki passed, and I took Levels Two and Three when the restrictions lifted. When I reached Level Three, I learned that I had a connection with repetitive patterns. I now understood that identifying things that need change is one part. We have to change what we believe about them, and to write a new story so that we do not repeat patterns that clearly do not work for us. We can make changes only when we become aware. I have always been empathetic towards others, the difference is that I am at peace inside, now. I wish to inspire others to open up and be at peace with themselves as well.

You can learn from whatever has happened in your life, and you can rise above it. Be honest with yourself about your true thoughts and feelings. I never liked hiding them. The therapeutic part of writing was always there for me, as I wrote my thoughts. No one talked about intuition. I had kept information hidden for so long; I was not aware of how deeply it affected me. Intuition has been an amazing tool for working on setting boundaries, repeating patterns and abuse. I can remember incidents and find ways to express experiences, then act to address the issues and give myself permission to live a happy life. I am working on what is important to me and feeling at peace. Peeling back the layers through the gifts of writing and intuition has revealed all *The Colours of Me!*

Holly Rose Holland is an intuitive author, international speaker, grief coach, former spouse, parent and grief survivor. While moving through the grief process herself, she noticed that people often become stuck when processing death, difficult relationships, employment-related issues, and even changes within themselves. She practises wellness through nature, natural products and intuition and travels to share her gifts with the world.

Holly's first book is called *Keep Moving, Creating a Life After Loss* (Sapphire Seahorse Press, 2020). Having always loved writing, she finds writing to be therapeutic for herself and others, as a means of expressing grief and creating a new life. Holly helps women get REAL: Remember, Express, Action, and Live.

This Crazy Journey Called 'Life'

by Jodie Satie

I believe our life experiences can shape us into who we are or will become. Some people will allow those life experiences to define who they become. Me, I am the sum total of lessons learnt along the way while experiencing all that life has offered to me thus far along the journey. I am a work in progress and ever-evolving masterpiece of humanity, femininity and creativity.

The earliest memories of my journey in life are as a shy little girl of divorced parents. The outcome of Mum and Dad divorcing was that we moved house more than the average family as Mum decided to make a fresh start by moving us to the country, first moving from Perth to Bunbury, and later to Esperance in Western Australia. With Mum being a single parent, I was often looked after by friends and I recall many early memories of being bullied by other kids because I was different and shy and lacked confidence. I was considered to be a fat child and was quite sensitive. I also felt innately that there was not abundance around me, and that money was tight. I remember going shopping with my grandmother one day and telling her that Mum had said she needed to buy me a pair of jeans. Of course, Mum didn't say any such thing, but I felt like Mum couldn't afford them and for some reason felt that my grandmother could – so I made up the story, got the jeans and felt like I was a 'normal' kid, and then got into trouble for telling fibs!!

What a ratbag I was. I learnt to read the situation and was a very perceptive child growing up. As a young child I felt loved, but equally I felt a lot of rejection due to all the moves, I attended many different schools, not staying in the one spot long enough to make any long-term lasting friendships, especially in my early years. At one stage I even lived with my grandmother while Mum and my stepfather started a new business seven hours and almost seven hundred kilometres north of Perth for a few months.

My real dad came to visit us randomly and very infrequently. I don't know that I really noticed too much at the time as we had a stepfather who had replaced the male father figure in our household. However, as I grew older, I always wondered why he didn't love us enough to keep in touch with us more often. When we did see him, we were told things such as he works and lives a long way away so can't come to see us very often, and then as a teenager I got told that Mum didn't know where he was. He had abandoned me. He used to shower us with gifts when we did see him though, so it was something to look forward to. To this day I will never know who told the truth and who told me stories in regard to contact with my real father in those early years. I've resigned myself to the fact that I will never know the real story and it was what it was – no more, no less.

I loved reading from an early age and by age seven I had read the entire Enid Blyton series and anything else I could get my hands on. I spent a lot of time on my own and filled this time in by reading. I was a curious child and loved to learn new things, so reading provided an answer to my curiosity and helped me fill in a lot of time. My early love of reading translated into my adult life and to this day I still enjoy a good book and getting lost in a great story, and I've always been good at spelling and was curious about language and eager to learn new words. If I didn't know what they meant I would look up their meaning – one more new word to add to my vocabulary, for that filing cabinet in my head!

In high school, while I was still being teased as I just never quite fitted in with the popular kids, I was fortunate to be able to travel overseas on a trip to England with my grandmother, during which time I developed a curiosity about the outside world along with a level of quiet confidence within myself. As I had been on a 'big trip away' the other kids at school thought I had returned home thinking I was better than them. Nothing could have been further from the truth! I came home from England six kilograms heavier, with some amazing experiences under my belt and a newfound interest in history and English castles and all things royal, but I still didn't fit in any better than I had when I left, and I felt fatter! I vowed to return to England though, and to this day I haven't made it back there, but I will!

Growing up, I worked part-time in my parents' roadhouse, even as a ten-year-old – well below the legal age I was allowed to, and I continued to develop confidence and learnt to read people from this experience. I was constantly getting told off by my parents for being too young to be serving behind the counter, however I was persistent! I became savvy with cash handling and developed customer service skills, learning to communicate with people from all walks of life. This experience was a valuable stepping stone into my adult life. I learnt to fake it till I made it, and exuded confidence, if that was what I needed to do to achieve an outcome. On the inside I don't think I've ever quite shaken that lack of confidence, but I've had plenty of practice at hiding it well.

At age seventeen and just five weeks prior to finishing my year 12 leaving examinations, I was fortunate to be offered a position as the clerk/typist at the Shire of Northampton. Living in a small town I had been taking the daily school bus the fifty-kilometre journey each way to school, and the offer of this job was something too good to refuse. I hated exams and my brain would turn to mush, no matter how much I studied, so this opportunity was even more enticing. The role entailed being the part-time librarian two afternoons a week, as well as an administrative all-rounder in a local government office, doing a variety of tasking including the banking, writing up the old rate registers and accompanying the Health Officer to vaccination clinics at the local hospital. It offered variety and a great stepping stone into adult life for me. A girl I knew a who was a year older than me had gone to Perth, studied and got qualifications and remained unemployed. I decided I wasn't going to follow her footsteps and risk being unemployed, so I gladly took this job that was being handed to me on a platter. I stayed there for two years, and then, encouraged by my mum who knew I had always wanted to work in a bank, I applied for jobs in banks. I had sent a few applications, with no luck, and was becoming quite disheartened, but Mum convinced me to keep trying, and to pursue my dreams, when all I wanted to do was give up. I got that bank job thanks to Mum's nagging and encouragement – that last letter that I didn't think would make any difference got me a job.

I moved to Geraldton and into a shared flat with a girl I knew from school. That lesson has stayed with me to this day. Never say never and just don't give up on your dreams.

When I was twenty I married the first man who really showed any interest in me, a schoolteacher from the big smoke – a most suitable choice. He was a good-looking, intelligent man who treated me well. The only option for me was to grab him with both hands; otherwise I might not get a second offer!

Working in the bank I was able to transfer back to Perth when he had finished doing his country service of three years in Geraldton, and my life was unfolding before me in a way that I was excited about. We moved to Perth, bought our own beautiful new home in a new and upcoming suburb, and planned a family. I worked in the bank for seven years before giving birth to the first of our two daughters.

I wanted to go back to work part-time in the bank, however back then work options were not as flexible as they are today, and there was no appetite for them to provide me with a part-time position. So, I resigned from my role in the bank and started to look for something that would enable me to work part-time and be at home with my daughter. Living in a newly established suburb, new community facilities were also being established and I was in the right place at the right time when a brand new local library and community centre was built. As I had worked part-time in a local library in my first working role, I was confident I could draw on that experience to get a part-time role with those skills at the new local library. The determination and focus within was drawn upon, I set my target and got a job as a library clerk. I stayed working there for nine years, working seventeen hours per week. I conducted weekly story times for local mums and babies and devised crafty activities for the same age group, coming up with ideas for Easter and Christmas and lots of themes in between. My creative side came out and I loved it. I got to meet lots of other local people, and had ready access to books, lots of them!

Ten years and two beautiful daughters later, that loneliness from my early childhood was still haunting me, and my husband and I had drifted in different directions. I wanted much more than I had and felt I wasn't going to achieve or experience it if I stayed put. I woke one day and with great clarity, packed my children and I up and fronted up on my parents' doorstep, where we stayed for six weeks.

My poor husband tried in vain to appeal to me to give it another go, but my mind was made up. I knew that I didn't want what I had; and was confident I could find what I was looking for.

I moved on, but still hadn't learnt my lessons and soon married again on the rebound into a disastrous relationship, ending up married to someone who was not my intellectual equal, nor was he a suitable stepfather. He was fun though, a bit of a daredevil, interesting, and wanted to be with me, unlike my ex-husband! It was enjoyable for a while but on the eve of our wedding that 'clarity' stopped by again and I thought, *What am I doing? I can't marry this man.* But next day I went ahead and did it anyway. I really should have learnt to listen to my inner feelings, my gut instinct, my intuition.

At this point in time, we needed the money. My husband earnt less than I did and most of it went on maintenance payments for his three children who lived with their mother. I had no other option, and both of my daughters were school age, so I pursued another role in a local council and began another adventure, this time working full-time.

A couple of years later a comment was made to me from a friend that she could see my eldest daughter might run away from home as she was so unhappy. I was told that my husband was psychologically abusive towards her. I couldn't believe that I could be so blind, that I didn't see this myself. What sort of a mother allows this to happen? That marriage too was left behind. Again, I drew on a hidden strength I hadn't realised that I possessed, but it was there when it was needed. I discovered I was a lot more capable than even I realised.

My local government service period from the Library, together with the current role, entitled me to take long service leave. With the combination of my marriage ending and the availability of a cashing out of my long service leave, I took the opportunity to run with my two daughters – Again!

Feelings of not liking my own company and that I needed to have a partner in my life to 'complete me' were still there though. I met someone who I had been introduced to by my ex-husband and who instantly I felt a connection with and was attracted to. We had even worked in the same organisation at the same time and had friends in common, but hadn't known one another within the previous ten years. We became a couple, and he was my third time lucky!

Five years after we were married and exactly ten years since his last reoccurrence, my husband was once again diagnosed with cancer, a tumour located in his sacrum. Fortunately, it had not metastasised and was able to be surgically removed, which entailed us putting our mortgage on hold at the bank and him being off work for three months to recover (including learning to walk again). Four very short years later, a random liver scan ordered by his GP revealed the cancer had returned and this time had metastasised to both his lungs. This resulted in a terminal diagnosis and the prognosis we were advised at the time was unknown. He could have two years, he could have five or ten, or he could live out the rest of his natural life. He has a Chondrosarcoma, a type of soft tissue bone cancer that is quite rare and mainly experienced by children.

The shock of hearing the word terminal was mind-blowing and during the weeks that followed we both walked around in what seemed to be a surreal and parallel universe. The uncertainty of it all was the hardest for me to comprehend. I could no longer plan ahead, or even think about retirement one day – because nothing was as it should have been for me/us any longer. What we previously knew no longer applied. When I talked to others about this no-one seemed to understand what I was talking about. I think this really is something that you need to have walked in my shoes to have understood. With some cancer counselling, we both came to learn, though, that life is in fact uncertain, and once we understood that, we gained a new perspective around our lives. The examples of any one of us just not waking up one morning, or of crossing the road and being run over by a bus – which could likely happen to any of us at any time – is the real uncertainty that we all face daily. It had never occurred to us before this time, that's all.

Sixteen years of marriage and three bouts of cancer later, I have developed an inner strength, wisdom and confidence to a level that I never knew existed. The cancer now terminal, my husband is a high-functioning alcoholic and I haven't stopped growing and developing myself, simply because I've had to on this journey. I had to grow – it has been 'sink or swim', and I've been swimming now for quite a while. My kids adore him, faults and all, and can talk to him if they feel they can't talk to me about something. He has been and is a calming influence on me and is the yin to my yang.

Through many experiences and lessons along the way I have learnt some incredibly valuable lessons including that what others think of me is none of my business; I have learnt that we all live with uncertainty in our lives each and every day – life is uncertain. I have learnt that the devil you know is better than the devil you don't. I have learnt that we need to be careful what comes out of our mouths as the universe provides for us in the most unexpected ways. I have learnt that each day is a gift, and we need to treat it as such – and to live in the moment. I have also learnt that 'this too shall pass' and tomorrow is a fresh brand new day of opportunity.

Early in this relationship I continued working full-time and ended up working in a government role working in ministerial liaison. It sounded exciting and interesting and highfalutin – and it absolutely has been. I have been working in government for more than sixteen years now in departments and in ministers' offices, and both my daughters have followed my footsteps and have secured good government roles both here and interstate. The experience working at this level of government has been remarkably stimulating and I continue to learn as I go, traversing the different government portfolios I find myself working in. It's primarily an administrative-based career, and very process-driven, however it provides that essential life balance for me. I can be process-driven and structured at work and release the creative side of my personality in my down time.

I discovered during 2020, a previously unrecognised joy in expressing my creativity, a creativity that I probably did know I had but hadn't given myself credit for. I have always pursued creative activities, whether they be craft or cross stitch or crotchet throughout my life, but most recently I have discovered acrylic painting, while in pursuit of finding something mindful to do to stop myself ruminating on the dysfunction in my life. The joy that can be found in creating a piece of art is something that can only be experienced by doing it for yourself. It has enabled me to release the 'control' factor within me, in determining how a picture will turn out. When you pour acrylic paint, it has a mind all of its own and there is no telling it to stay within the lines or to create a specific pattern –the ability to 'go with the flow' takes over and *voila!* a masterpiece is magically created. This has been a wonderfully exciting lesson for me.

As a mother of two adult daughters, I have learnt that our children don't always turn out to be who we want or expect them to be, and they certainly don't necessarily turn out to be anything like who we are as a person. They inherit our gene pool, but not our beliefs or ideas. I am learning to embrace and accept this and them for who they are … As a nanna I am experiencing the joy of loving a new little person, whom I have only a small window of opportunity to influence, while also getting used to the fact that I'm only Nanna. The 'control' personality within me just wants to take over caring for her, to keep her protected in a cocoon of cotton wool where she can't be hurt or bruised or affected by the big bad world out there.

As the daughter of a mother who is now eighty-two, I have learnt as I have gotten older, that a little patience and understanding goes much further when relating to my mum now more than it ever did. It probably wouldn't have hurt if I had had this outlook thirty years ago, however I guess maturity and wisdom come with age. Poor Mum, I always thought it was her fault when things went wrong in my life, as 'I got it from my mum' was a common saying I used when defending myself to my first husband. Now I have lived some of that life experience and knowledge and understand that Mum did the very best in bringing me and my brother up, with what she had and the knowledge she had at the time – just as I have done with my own daughters.

None of us set out when we get married to think that we will get divorced or anticipate the road that lies ahead. We all think 'for better or for worse, in sickness and in health … 'til death do us part …' and that's our lot until we leave this earth. Life doesn't always turn out how we expect it to be, it throws us curve balls and lessons to deal with, and we either roll with it and adapt or we don't. I'm currently rolling and adapting a lot more than I used to, dodging those damn curve balls!

Jodie Satie is a fifty-six-year-old Western Australian, born and bred. She is married to Erik and lives in Perth. Jodie has two daughters, a stepson and a stepdaughter, and a granddaughter Zoe, who she absolutely adores.

Always an avid reader and interested in life and being the best it can be, she enjoys travelling the world, walking, spending time with her two dogs, eating good food and learning. A lifelong learner, each day is an opportunity to learn something new. 'Never say never' is Jodie's motto.

Purpose.

Do not forget who you are, and where you come from. You are made from the brightest stars and the widest oceans. You are made of the highest mountains and the tallest trees. You are made of magic and dreams, wishes and light. You have heroes, warriors, kings and queens, gods and goddesses flowing through your veins. You come from infinite possibilities and incredible odds. You are here for a reason.

— *Walk the Earth*

www.ingramcontent.com/pod-product-compliance
Lightning Source LLC
Chambersburg PA
CBHW031243290426
44109CB00012B/420